FOUR SEASONS GARDENING

Better Homes and Gardens®

FOUR SEASONS GARDENING

*A
month-by-month
guide
to planning, planting,
and caring
for your garden*

Ann Reilly Dines

BETTER HOMES AND GARDENS® BOOKS
Des Moines

BETTER HOMES AND GARDENS® BOOKS
An Imprint of Meredith® Books

President, Book Group: Joseph J. Ward
Vice President and Editorial Director: Elizabeth P. Rice
Art Director: Ernest Shelton

FOUR SEASONS GARDENING
was prepared and produced by
Michael Friedman Publishing Group, Inc.
15 West 26th Street
New York, New York 10010

Editor: Kelly Matthews
Art Direction: Lynne Yeamans
Designer: Jan Melchior
Photography Editor: Emilya Naymark

Library of Congress Catalog Card Number 94-75967

ISBN 0-696-04648-2

Color separations by Bright Arts (H.K.) Ltd.
Printed in China by Leefung-Asco Printers Ltd.

TO ALAN

MY HUSBAND, MY PARTNER,

MY PATIENT FRIEND

Thanks to Ball Seed Co., West Chicago, IL; Park Seed Co., Greenwood, SC; National Garden Bureau, Downer's Grove, IL; Nassau County Cooperative Extension Association, Plainview, NY; American Rose Society, Shreveport, LA; Dr. Jerry Pepin, Pickseed West, Tangent, OR; Netherlands Flower Bulb Information Center, Brooklyn, NY; DeVor Roses, Freedom, CA; Peto Seed Co., Saticoy, CA.

CONTENTS

PART III

Seasonal Timetables

Appendix

INTRODUCTION

When planning the garden, consider complementary sizes and shapes such as this striking combination of majestic foxgloves and lower-growing primulas.

A unique combination of art and science, gardening requires knowledge not only of how to design, create, and maintain a beautiful landscape but also of when to do it. This book covers both aspects of gardening, but with an emphasis on the when. It explains how to sow seeds—and discusses the right time for sowing. You'll learn when to plant, when to prune, when to water, and when to fertilize. The result will be a garden you can enjoy and be proud of—with the least amount of effort.

Keep in mind, however, that the information given here should be used as guidelines, not followed as strict rules. Weather patterns fluctuate, for example, and the temperature in your area may be cooler or warmer than average, forcing you to make adjustments in your gardening schedule. Or, you may garden in a microclimate, which could change your gardening timetable by several weeks from that of a friend who gardens only a mile away. Or perhaps water is scarce in your area, and you need to adjust your planting schedule so that you're adding plants to the garden during the rainy season. No matter what special needs your garden may have, remember to follow all timetables and suggestions with an eye toward flexibility, tailoring them to suit your situation.

Whatever the case, your garden is certain to be a one-of-a-kind creation, one that reflects your personality. For that reason, it is important to also keep your own annual records, noting what did and did not work for you. As your garden grows to its lush and productive best, so too will your knowledge of both the art and science of gardening with the help of your personal maintenance calendar, hands-on experience, and the information found on the following pages.

8

9

PART I

GARDENING
FUNDAMENTALS

Whether you garden in a rural environment or

in a postage stamp–size backyard of a city town house,

the following gardening fundamentals are essential to

creating a garden that will flourish and thrive.

Be sure to carefully review these general guidelines for

growing healthy plants; the information contained

here will be useful as you turn to the remaining sections of

this book and will often be used as a reference.

TOOLS AND HARDWARE

No matter what gardening task you set out to perform, it will be to your advantage to have the right tool for the job; this will make the job easier as well as more enjoyable. When you shop for tools, however, remember that the least expensive may not be the best buy in the long run; a good-quality tool may be more expensive, but it will last for years. When selecting a tool, hold it in your hand to make sure that it fits comfortably and it's not too heavy. You might consider shopping for tools in the autumn or winter; the prices may be better and you'll have time to comparison shop.

Always keep your tools in good condition. Clean them after every use, oil them frequently to keep rust from forming, and promptly remove any rust that does form. In winter, when there isn't much to do outdoors, check all tools for necessary repairs, then clean and oil them. Tools used for cutting should be sharpened at this time as well.

A well-equipped gardener has all the right tools
at hand to ease the work of garden chores.

Although some gardening tools may be considered non-essential, others are indispensable. A trowel, for example, is necessary for planting small plants such as annuals, small perennials, vegetables, herbs, and

bulbs. Trowels come in several different widths depending on your needs. If you need to create small round holes, purchase a bulb planter, which you can use

for planting any small plant not just bulbs.

To plant trees, shrubs, and other large plants and to prepare and move soil, you will need a shovel. Shovels come in different handle lengths, so you should be able to find one that suits your height. Similar to shovels but with blades that have a flat rather than rounded bottom edge, spades are used for digging, preparing soil, root pruning, and edging.

A spading fork is similar in shape to a spade, but has rigid tines instead of a blade. Spading forks are handy for digging perennials and bulbs that need dividing, as well as for digging up large plants for transplanting. The tines also can break up large clumps of soil, as well as aerate small lawn areas.

Pruning shears are necessary for cutting stems (up to the thickness of your little finger) and for removing dead flowers from woody plants. There are two types of pruning shears: the hook and blade type, which has two curved cutting surfaces, and the anvil type, which has one—a cutting blade that is pushed against a flat surface. The anvil type crushes rather than cuts soft stems and therefore isn't usually recommended.

For cutting branches thicker than pruning shears can handle, you will need lopping shears or a saw. Loppers have long handles so you can reach high branches without having to climb a ladder. If you need to use a saw for thick branches, choose a pruning saw with a wide-toothed pattern, not a carpenter's saw. For heavy work, buy or rent a chain saw.

Hedge clippers with long blades make trimming hedges quick work, but don't use them to cut through thick stems or branches. For this or for trimming large hedges, life is easier with a power hedge clipper.

Unless you hire someone to cut your lawn, you will need a lawn mower. An old-fashioned push type is fine for small areas, but most gardeners find electric or gas mowers much easier to use. Electric mowers have some drawbacks, however, such as limiting your mowing range to the length of the extension cord. For very large lawns—over a half acre or so—a riding mower is almost a necessity.

Other essentials for a manicured lawn include grass shears for trimming edges and corners that the lawn mower cannot reach and a hand-operated or

13

power edger to trim along the sidewalk or driveway. Many gardeners, however, find that string trimmers are easier to use than grass shears. For seeding and applying lawn fertilizers, spreaders do a much better job than you'll be able to do by hand. Spreaders have garden uses, but usually are relegated to lawn work. Look for one with a plastic hopper; the metal types rust and clog easily.

You'll need a rake with flexible metal or plastic tines to rake leaves from the lawn or remove debris from beds and borders. If you are seeding a lawn, vegetables, or annuals, you will need a rake with rigid tines to level and smooth the soil. There also are special rakes to remove thatch from the lawn.

You can pull weeds by hand, but the task is easier in large areas if you have a hoe. Keep the blade sharp so that when you pull the hoe toward you, it will cut the weeds. Hoes have short or long handles; using one with a long handle eliminates bending and kneeling down. Deep-rooted weeds can be removed with an asparagus knife, which, as the name suggests, also is used to harvest asparagus.

14

The right shovel (ABOVE) can ease potentially backbreaking work. Keep lawn-weeding tools (BELOW) clean and sharp to ensure their efficiency.

SOIL

Almost without exception, you cannot grow a good, healthy garden if you do not have good, healthy soil. If you are faced with soil that is less than ideal, do not despair, because with the proper improvements, it still can grow robust flowers and fruit.

Before you can improve your soil, however, you have to understand its composition. Besides organic matter, water, and air, soil is made up of mineral particles, namely clay, silt, and sand. Clay is the smallest particle, and clay soils have a dense structure and fine texture. They are heavy soils; the particles tend to stick together, causing poor drainage and inadequate aeration. Sand is the largest particle; sandy soils have loose structure and coarse texture. They drain well and have excellent aeration but do not retain moisture and nutrients well. Silty soils fall between clay soils and sandy soils. The ideal soil is a mixture of all three particles and is called loam. Loam holds nutrients, retains water but still drains well, and has good aeration, which encourages root growth. Unfortunately, loam rarely occurs in nature.

To create loamlike soil conditions, organic matter must be added. In sandy soil, organic matter increases moisture and nutrient-retaining capabilities; in clay soil, it improves drainage and aeration. If you are skeptical about the importance of organic matter, try growing identical plants side by side in improved and unimproved soil. You will never doubt the importance of organic matter again.

When a soil is high in organic matter, it is said to be rich; low in organic matter, it is known as poor soil. Organic matter, sometimes called humus, can be added to the soil in several forms: sphagnum peat moss, leaf mold, dried manure, aged wood chips or sawdust, or compost. You can make compost from garden debris and kitchen scraps. Add enough organic matter so the final soil is approximately 25 per-cent organic matter; how much you add depends on the original condition of the soil. Fortunately, it is hard to overdo organic matter.

Clay soils also can be improved with gypsum, which is calcium sulfate. It binds the clay particles together, adds calcium to the soil, and removes excess salt, but otherwise does not change the soil. It can be added at any time of year but is best done in autumn or spring, before planting.

One other important aspect of your soil is pH, which is the measure of the acidity or alkalinity of your soil. Measured on a scale of 1.0 to 14.0 with 7.0 being neutral, a pH below 7.0 indicates an acid soil and a pH above 7.0 indicates an alkaline soil. The ideal pH for most plants is 5.0 to 7.5; notable exceptions are broad-leaved evergreens and blueberries, which prefer a pH of 4.5 to 5.0.

If the pH of your soil is not correct, plants will not grow

15

well; soil nutrients become locked up, making them unavailable for absorption by the roots. Limestone is best for raising pH, and dolomitic limestone is most recommended because it is slow acting and contains magnesium,

Ideal soil, called loam, is the perfect mixture of sand, clay, and silt.

an essential element for plant growth. To lower pH, sulfur is recommended. However, because organic matter generally is acidic and most fertilizers are too, their addition may adjust your soil's pH by themselves if it is only slightly alkaline. No matter what product you use to adjust soil pH, follow label directions.

Because it is impossible to determine the pH of your soil by looking at it, it is a good idea to test the pH before making any moves. You can do this yourself with a pH test kit, which is available at garden centers, or by collecting a quart sample of the soil and taking it to a commercial laboratory or your county extension agent. Many soil tests determine pH only, but you can request a complete analysis from a soil lab, which will also determine organic matter and nutrient levels. This is a good idea if you suspect you have problem soil.

Soil improvement and preparation is a matter of correct timing, because the soil structure can be ruined if the soil is too wet. To test for the correct conditions, take a handful of soil and squeeze it together. If it forms a solid ball, let the soil dry out a bit before working it. If it crumbles, it is ready.

Soil should be improved to the depth the roots will grow. This means 8 to 12 inches for annuals, bulbs, perennials, vegetables, and herbs, and 24 inches for roses, shrubs, and trees. Dig out the planting area, and add enough organic matter so it makes up 25 percent of the final soil mix. Depending on the time of year, you may or may not be able to add other soil amendments when improving your soil.

Soil can be improved in the spring before planting or during the previous autumn. If possible, it's better to improve soil in the autumn, which will give it time to settle over the winter. If you are improving soil the previous autumn, add a complete fertilizer at that time (see the information on fertilizers later in part one). If soil preparation is done in spring, add a complete fertilizer only if you are improving the soil one month or more before planting. Otherwise, add a fertilizer high in phosphorus, such as superphosphate or bonemeal, then use a complete fertilizer once the plants are established. If you need to adjust the pH and add fertilizer, adjust the pH at least one month before fertilizing. That way the soil can make the best use of the nutrients.

Other soil problems creep up from time to time, especially in alkaline soils. If plants become chlorotic, a condition that causes plant leaves to yellow, lower the pH or add iron. If salt builds up, water slowly and deeply and add gypsum. In areas where soil is so poor and infertile that it is almost impossible to improve it or if drainage is bad and cannot be easily corrected, it is better to build raised beds.

16

PLANTING

Once the soil, the foundation of your garden, has been improved, it is time to plant. This is an exciting time for gardeners, as they wait with great expectation for their plants to begin to grow.

Although there are minor differences in planting techniques depending on the type of plant, there is one basic rule to follow that will ensure that the plants have every opportunity to flourish: They should start their lives in the garden in good homes. In other words, dig an ample hole that will allow the roots to be surrounded with good soil to grow in. Plants should never simply be pushed into the ground.

When planted properly in good soil, plant roots will be healthier and the garden will thrive.

WOODY PLANTS

Woody plants, whether they are shrubs, trees, roses, or vines, can be purchased, ready to plant, in one of three ways: bare root, containerized, or balled and burlapped (B&B). Bare-root plants are dormant and have no soil around the roots (although there may be a protective covering). These most often are acquired from mail-order nurseries and must be planted in the spring or, if winter temperatures do not fall below 0°F, in autumn, when plants are not in active growth.

If bare-root plants cannot be planted immediately, keep them in a cool, dark place so they will not start to grow, and wrap the roots in wet peat moss or newspaper to keep them moist. A day or two before planting, soak the roots in a bucket of plain water, adding a small amount of liquid fertilizer to the water, if you desire. After the hole has been dug, fill it with a cone of improved soil, adding enough so the crown of the plant will be at soil level after planting. Place the plant in the hole, and spread out the roots so they are evenly distributed over the cone (any roots that are extremely long, broken,

Once a container has been removed for planting (ABOVE), it is important not to disturb the plant's roots. A popular bedding plant, coleus (RIGHT) is an annual that requires little additional care after planting.

or damaged should be pruned first). Fill the hole about two-thirds full with soil, gently tamping it down, then fill the hole with water. After the water has drained, fill the hole to the top with soil and water again. Mounding soil over the base of the plant until growth starts will keep the stems from drying out.

Containerized plants may be in plastic, metal, paper, or compressed-peat pots. Whatever the material, the container should be removed before planting, even if the label states that it is plantable. This allows for better and faster root growth into the surrounding soil. Dig a hole about twice the width of the container, and test the depth to be sure it is correct. Remove the container as careful-

ly as possible to avoid disturbing the roots; turn the plant upside down and tap the container until it pulls off or cut the container away with shears. Fill the hole two-thirds full with soil, add water, and after the water has drained off, fill the hole to the top with soil and water again.

B&B plants are planted much the same way as containerized plants, except that the burlap is not completely removed (any plastic over the burlap, however, must be taken off). Once the plant is in position in the hole, cut the strings holding the burlap and pull the burlap back.

Containerized and B&B plants can be added to the ground any time the soil is workable from early spring until

late autumn, but try to avoid summer planting. Otherwise, you'll have to give the plants a lot of tender loving care. The cool days of autumn are best, because all the plant's energy can go into root production, provided winter temperatures do not drop below 0°F. Evergreens should be planted earlier in autumn than deciduous plants so that their roots can become established before cold weather; otherwise, they may desiccate too much and die.

Deciduous plants should be pruned back after planting to force strength into the roots.

Prune off about one-third of the branches, taking the time also to shape the plants. Evergreen plants usually are not pruned at planting time unless trimming is needed.

Trees will need to be staked at planting time. Use two stakes if the diameter of the trunk is less than 3 inches, and three stakes or guy wires if the diameter is greater than that. Set the stakes into the ground just beyond the root ball, and leave them there for at least a year. Tree trunks also should be wrapped in burlap or tape for a year or two until a thick bark develops to prevent sunscald.

BEDDING PLANTS

Bedding plants are nonwoody plants such as annuals, vegetables, perennials, biennials, and herbs. Keep them outdoors in their containers in a partially shaded place until you're ready to plant them, and check them every day to see if they need to be watered. When you're ready to plant, water the plants, as well as the ground they will be calling home. Carefully remove the plants from the flats or other containers by turning them upside down, rapping or squeezing the container, if necessary,

19

until they slip out. With a trowel, dig a hole about twice the size of the root ball, and place the plant in the hole, making certain that the base of the plant will be at the level it grew before and gently firming up the soil around

ground. If the plants were grown in peat pots, peel away as much of the pot as possible and plant the rest, making sure that the lip of the pot is below the soil level.

Perennials can be planted in early to midspring, as soon as the

help them survive the heat and transplant shock. Perennial herbs are planted following the same schedule as other perennials. Biennials are planted in the autumn for bloom the following spring or in very early spring for bloom that same year.

The planting timing of annual flowers, vegetables, and herbs depends on the type of plant, as well as the weather. Very hardy plants can be planted as soon as the soil can be worked in late winter or early spring. Hardy plants are planted a little later, about four weeks before the last frost. Half-hardy and tender plants must not go into the ground until after all danger of frost has passed. Tender, warm-season annual flowers and vegetables also need warm soil to grow well, so it is best to wait a little longer to plant them. Hardy and very hardy plants also can be added to the garden in late summer and autumn for autumn and winter color or harvest.

Beds designed to highlight hot-colored flowers benefit from the cooling additions of companion plants. Here, silvery dusty-miller and low, mounding alyssum break up the intense color scheme created by the zinnias and salvia.

the roots. Water well, and again daily until new growth starts.

When planting bedding plants, handle them only by the leaves so you don't damage the delicate stems. If roots are compacted, spread them apart slightly before placing the plants in the

soil can be worked, or in the autumn (the exceptions to this are Oriental poppies, peonies, and irises, which must be planted in the autumn for them to bloom their first year). Containerized perennials can be planted all summer, provided care is given to

If you garden in a cool area, you can extend the season by covering young, warmth-loving plants with plastic film after planting. If you don't, you may not have enough growing time to make it worth the effort.

20

BULBS

Bulbs that bloom in the spring are planted the previous autumn, while those that bloom in summer usually are planted in spring after all danger of frost has passed. There are two ways to plant bulbs: You can dig individual holes into prepared soil and set the bulbs at the bottom of the holes, or you can dig out an entire bed, place the bulbs in the bottom, and cover the bulbs with soil. The second method is easier if you have a large number to plant in one area.

Always keep an eye on new plantings and be sure to water them as needed until they show signs of new and strong growth. Anything planted in autumn should have one good watering after planting, and then it probably won't need another substantial watering until the following spring.

TRANSPLANTING

The transplanting of plants from one area of the garden to another often is a necessity of gardening life. When digging up the plants, be careful to disturb the roots as little as possible, lifting the plant gingerly from the ground with a spade or a spading fork. Make sure to replant it as soon as possible, moving the plant carefully to avoid damaging it. From that point on, follow the planting guidelines already mentioned, treating the transplant as if it were a new acquisition.

Perennials, including herbs, are transplanted in spring when growth starts or in early autumn, except for Oriental poppies, peonies, and irises, which should be transplanted in autumn. Evergreens should be moved in midspring or early to midautumn. All deciduous plants should be moved only after they have lost their leaves and are dormant. Bulbs should be transplanted after they bloom and the foliage starts to die down. Although it's possible to transplant in summer, the risk of damaging or destroying the plant is high, because it probably won't survive the shock of transplanting when coupled with summer's sun and heat.

With globular purple flowers that bloom in late spring, giant onions (ABOVE RIGHT) are best planted the previous autumn. Grown from bulbs, checkered lilies (RIGHT) have unusually shaped flowers.

WATERING

Some plants have an incredible ability to withstand periods without rainfall or supplemental watering, but for the most part you will need to pay attention to your garden's watering needs for it to thrive. Several factors are important here. There may simply be a shortage of rainfall, for example. High heat or wind also will cause plants to dry out more quickly, necessitating extra watering unless protected by shade or wind screens. Sandy soil will need more water than heavy clay soil; proper improvement of the soil, however, will reduce watering needs. The roots of large trees may rob nearby plants of soil moisture, as will weeds. With these factors in mind, water as needed, keep the soil weed-free, and install a mulch (see the information on mulches later in part one) to retain moisture in the soil.

You will note that plants' water requirements are given throughout this book. Study this information before selecting plants for your garden, especially if your garden's moisture level is above or below normal or if water is scarce and watering will be difficult.

Always encourage deep rooting by watering deeply and as infrequently as possible. The worst thing you can do for a plant is encourage shallow roots, because it will not be as healthy or as able to withstand winds or periods of drought. There are several clues that will let you know if the garden needs watering. If the top inch of the soil is dry or if leaves show signs of wilting, it is time to get out the watering can or the hose.

Another good rule of thumb is to apply 1 inch of water per week if the garden has average requirements, adjusting the amount of water applied according to your garden's needs. To determine how to apply an inch of water, first use a simple rain gauge to measure how much rain falls from the sky during the course of one week. Next, place your rain gauge halfway between the sprinkler and the farthest point that the water reaches, and time how long the sprinkler needs to run to deliver an inch of water. If $\frac{1}{2}$ inch of rain has fallen during the week, run the sprinkler for half the amount of time it needs to deliver an inch of water to make up the other $\frac{1}{2}$ inch. Use similar testing methods if you water the garden by hand or drip irrigation.

There are several methods of watering a garden. Drip irrigation makes the most efficient use of water, although it does take longer to water. It delivers water to the ground only, where it is needed, does not get foliage and flowers wet, and is not as affected by wind, as sprinklers are. Soaker hoses, which are laid on the ground, work in much the same way, but sometimes deliver water where it isn't needed.

Sprinklers, which may be oscillating or rotating, are a popular way of watering, but overlap is sometimes unavoidable and

22

any water that falls on the sidewalk or driveway is wasted. Sprinklers come in different sizes, so choose one that matches your needs. Because flowers and foliage get wet with this type of watering, try to use sprinklers in created, so the ground will not have to be dug up later on. If you are thinking of using this method, choose one that works on a soil-moisture sensor, not a timer, or you'll find your sprinklers running in the rain or when doesn't. Hand watering is the best method to use where there are water shortages, because you can apply water only to the plants that need it.

When purchasing a hose, buy one that is unlikely to kink; rein-

Using a hose with a spray-nozzle attachment to hand water is ideal for small gardens or for spot watering. When watering from overhead, however, it is best to water early in the day so that the foliage and flowers will have time to dry out.

the morning so the plants have time to dry out. In addition, avoid watering on a windy day; too much water will be wasted.

Automatic sprinkler systems are more worry-free. These are best installed when the garden is the garden does not need water.

Hand watering with a hose or a watering can is time consuming but a necessity when watering seed beds, containers, or small transplants that need water when the rest of the garden forced plastic is the best. Different types of nozzles also are available, depending on the fineness of the spray you want. To prevent waste, be sure to shut the water off after each use and repair any leaks as soon as they appear. For safety's as well as appearance's sakes, roll up the hose after you've finished watering. If you won't need the hose over the winter, be sure to drain it in late autumn.

23

FERTILIZERS AND FERTILIZING

Plants, just like the gardeners who grow them, need food to survive, grow, and flourish. Although soil, water, and air provide plants with some nutrition, fertilizer almost always is a necessity. When feeding plants, it is important not only to give them the right fertilizer but also to apply it at the right time, which is when they are growing, flowering, and forming fruit.

When you read a fertilizer label, you'll notice a set of three numbers, such as 5–10–5 or 20–20–20. These represent the percentages found in the fertilizer of the three basic elements needed for plant growth: nitrogen, phosphorus, and potassium. Nitrogen is needed for stem and leaf growth and deep green color. Phosphorus stimulates root growth and photosynthesis, and promotes flowering and fruiting. Potassium is necessary for a healthy metabolism and aids in winter hardiness and disease resistance. When all three of these elements are present, the fertilizer is said to be balanced or complete.

Ten other elements—boron, calcium, chlorine, copper, iron, magnesium, manganese, molybdenum, sulfur, and zinc—also are needed for plant growth; these are known as minor or trace elements. Most are available in soil, air, and water, but occasionally supplemental calcium, magnesium, sulfur, or iron is needed. If a plant shows signs of poor growth or has discolored leaves, it may be deficient in a trace element.

The source of the nitrogen and, to some extent, the other elements in a fertilizer determine if it is organic or inorganic. Organic, or natural, fertilizers include bonemeal, cottonseed meal, sewage sludge, and blood meal, among others. The percentage of nutrients in organic fertilizers usually is lower than in inorganic ones, and they are bulky; however, they also are slow acting and not as likely to burn plants. It is important not to confuse organic fertilizers

A good organic source of calcium, limestone provides plants with this essential trace element as well as raises the pH of the soil.

24

with organic soil amendments. Organic soil amendments are almost a necessity for good plant growth; the choice of organic versus inorganic fertilizers is not as important, except to the determined organic gardener.

Inorganic fertilizers are mineral salts and include such products as potassium nitrate and potassium phosphate. They are more water soluble than most organic fertilizers and, therefore, are quicker acting. If misapplied, however, they can burn plants, and they leach from the soil rapidly, especially if it is sandy.

Slow-release fertilizers, which release nutrients over a period of time, are available. Some are activated by moisture, others by temperature. They are beneficial to the busy gardener because they need to be applied less often; one feeding in the beginning of the season will last until the same time next year.

Fertilizers are available in liquid and dry forms. Liquid fertilizers are fast acting and are good for container plants and to give plants a boost, especially at flowering time. They do not last long in the soil, however, and need to be applied often. Dry fertilizers can be slow acting or fast acting. Fast-acting fertilizers have the same characteristics as liquid fertilizers; slow-acting ones need to be used less often. Fertilizers in solution can be applied to foliage, but sometimes burning occurs, so test a few leaves before applying to entire plants.

The type of fertilizer you choose depends on the plant you are feeding. Lawns and foliage plants benefit from fertilizers high in nitrogen, such as 10–6–4 or 23–7–7. Flowering and fruiting plants need a fertilizer where the nitrogen is not in the highest percentage; these include 5–10–5 or 5–10–10. If a complete fertilizer is not added to the soil at planting time, one high in phosphorus, such as bonemeal or superphosphate (0–45–0), should be used at that time.

The timing of fertilizer application is most important, because food must be in the soil ready for absorption by roots when the plant is growing, flowering, and fruiting. If possible, incorporate a complete fertilizer into the soil when you prepare. If the soil is prepared less than a month before planting time, incorporate only phosphorus, to promote root growth, and feed with a complete fertilizer once the plants are established. Annuals and vegetables may need more than one feeding a year; use your own judgment based on how healthy the plants look and how well they are growing. Trees and shrubs need feeding once a year when growth is most active; perennials should be fed in spring when growth starts. Bulbs should be fertilized when the foliage starts to brown after flowering is finished. Roses are heavy feeders and need fertilizing several times each growing season.

If you garden in an area where water is scarce and you rely on rainfall, adjust your fertilizing schedule so you fertilize during the rainy season if at all possible.

Many plant experts recommend dormant feeding, which is the application of fertilizer to plants in late autumn or winter when they are not growing. As long as the soil does not drop below 40°F, the roots will absorb fertilizer and be used by the plant as soon as growth starts. This is useful for trees, shrubs, and lawns. If you dormant feed, do not reapply fertilizer in early spring.

Apply fertilizer to moist soil over the ground that covers the plant's roots, and soak the area well with water. Follow label directions regarding how much to apply; the amount varies with the formulation.

25

WEEDS
AND WEEDING

A weed is a plant that grows where you don't want it to. It is essential to keep weeds out of the garden, because they rob water, nutrients, and sometimes light from the plants you are striving to grow. Aggressive weeds can smother an ornamental planting or take over a fine lawn. In addition, many insects and diseases breed and overwinter in weeds.

If you have a lot of weeds, it may be a sign of other problems. Weeds seem to thrive in poor

In lieu of treating a lawn with a chemical herbicide, there are several products on the market that will facilitate lawn weed removal on a small scale.

soil or in soil that is compacted, of the wrong pH, improperly fertilized, improperly watered, or draining improperly. Look at this as a sign that you may need to take other corrective actions besides eliminating the weeds.

If there are only a few weeds, they can be pulled by hand or with a hoe. In large areas, however, it is easier to treat them with a weed killer, or herbicide. These come in various types and their selection depends upon the weed you want to eliminate.

Some chemical herbicides kill everything they come in contact with, including beneficial plants, so use these only if you are renovating a large area. They vary in the length of their efficacy, so read the label carefully: With some, you can

replant in a week, and with others, it might be six months.

Herbicides that prevent weed seeds from germinating are known as pre-emergent herbicides. These are used mostly with grassy weeds. The timing of their application is critical because they must be in the soil before the weed seeds start to grow. Most will not damage other plants, but read the label to be sure. Some will prevent flower and lawn grass seeds from germinating, so again be sure you are buying what suits your needs.

Herbicides applied to actively growing plants are known as post-emergent herbicides. These are most effective if applied to weeds when they are still immature. Be careful when using these, however, because they can damage ornamental plants. Spot treatment is safer, although large areas can be treated with a spreader or sprayer if no beneficial plants will be affected. Always read the label, and never apply herbicides on a windy day.

26

MULCH
AND MULCHING

A mulch is a carpet of loose material placed on top of soil. Mulches can be organic or inorganic, and both have many benefits. They keep the soil cool during warm weather and warm when the weather is cool, and help the soil maintain a more even temperature during each season. Mulches also help the soil retain moisture, reducing watering needs. They help to keep weeds from sprouting and reduce soil blowing and erosion. Mulches prevent mud from splattering during rainfall or watering and, therefore, assist in reducing diseases. Organic mulches also add beneficial organisms to the soil as they decompose.

Many products are used for mulch. Hulls, bark chips, leaf mold, gravel, and black plastic are just a few examples. What you choose is a matter of personal taste and depends on the look you want to achieve and what is locally available. As you shop around, keep in mind the aesthetics of a mulch, as well as its other benefits.

A loose covering of hay mulch will help keep weeds down and soil at an even temperature.

The timing of mulch application depends on your goals. Applied in early spring, mulch keeps the ground cool. If you live in a cool area and want to grow warm-season annuals and vegetables, do not apply mulch until the ground has warmed up; otherwise, the soil will be too cool for those plants. If soil temperature is not critical, apply mulch once a year in spring or early summer. The mulch from the previous year can be left in place, then covered over with a new layer; or you can work mulch into the soil, then add the new.

The term "winter mulch" refers to winter protection and is discussed later in part one.

27

PRUNING

Sometimes it may seem difficult to take pruning shears in hand and cut away live growth from a plant, but there are many good reasons to do so. Pruning encourages new growth, keeps plants dense, and can actually improve flowering and fruiting. It also controls a plant's size, directs its growth, and gives it a better shape. On a less aesthetic note, pruning is necessary to remove dead, diseased, or damaged branches, to remove branches that are growing too near the house or utility wires, or to remove suckers that appear from the understock. Roots as well as plant tops can be pruned; this usually is done in preparation for transplanting.

Reread the earlier section on tools and hardware to refresh your knowledge about pruning shears and other implements. Be sure to keep shears clean and sharp and to disinfect them with alcohol or bleach if you prune a diseased plant.

When you prune stems, always cut about $1/4$ inch above a bud, preferably an outward-facing bud. Cut at a 45-degree angle slanted away from the bottom of the bud. No matter what kind of plant you are pruning, never leave a stub on a branch.

Whether thinned with a hand pruner (OPPOSITE TOP), handsaw (OPPOSITE CENTER), or lopper (OPPOSITE BOTTOM), a well-pruned tree, such as this apple (RIGHT), is a healthier tree. Cutting excess growth will improve flowering, fruiting, and the tree's looks.

Shrubs may or may not need annual pruning. If their size and shape is acceptable to you and there are no dead or damaged stems to remove, you don't need to do anything. Dead or damaged branches can be cut away any time, but it is easier when there are no leaves on the plant. Any weak or crowded growth can be removed at this time also. The general shaping of shrubs follows one simple rule: Prune spring-flowering shrubs after they bloom, and summer-flowering shrubs before they bloom.

Overgrown deciduous shrubs should be rejuvenated over a three-year period by removing

one-third of the growth each year, cutting the branches to the ground. It is almost impossible to rejuvenate an overgrown evergreen, so it is best not to let it get into this condition in the first place. To keep evergreens in good condition, give them an annual pruning if they need shaping or to encourage dense growth. This should be done each year in spring when the plants are in active growth.

28

Hedges should be sheared so their bottom is wider than their top. This ensures that the bottom receives light and does not die off. Prune hedges one or more times a year depending on the formality you desire. Pruning is best done in spring before or during growth.

New deciduous trees usually need some pruning so they will develop strength and grow into the shape you want. Any weak, dead, or damaged branches should be removed, as well as branches that cross each other or grow into the center of the plant. Make sure the tree has only one leader, or growing tip, and if necessary, prune around the trunk to make sure the branches are balanced and not growing too closely together. As the tree grows, check to see if it needs any more pruning and shape it as needed, removing any weak crotches and cutting off any branches that are too close to the ground. This can be done at almost any time of year.

Young evergreens don't need as much pruning. Make sure that there is only one leader and that the plant is growing compactly and in the shape you want. Prune junipers, arborvitaes, and yews before growth starts, and

29

pines, firs, spruces, and hemlocks after growth has begun.

Mature trees need pruning to remove dead or diseased branches, to remove branches that are growing too close to the house or utility lines, to allow more light to reach the garden below, or to control the size and shape of the tree. Pruning can be done at any time of year, but it's easier to do in the late autumn through early spring when no leaves are on the tree and you can see what you're doing. The main exceptions to this are maple, birch, and beech, which bleed when cut and therefore should be pruned in late spring or early summer. If a tree flowers and you don't want to forsake this year's blooms, wait until flowering is over to prune it. Never cut off a large branch with a single cut. Instead, use this three-cut sequence: 1) Make a cut on the underside of the branch about halfway through about 15 inches from the trunk; this prevents bark from tearing later. 2) Cut from the top side all the way through the branch about 4 inches out from the first cut. 3) Cut the stub off, making sure to leave the bark ridge and the branch collar intact. Trim the bark around the cut with a knife to speed healing.

Although old garden roses may not need a lot of pruning, modern roses do or they will not grow and bloom well. Each year, roses need to be pruned in late winter to early spring when the buds start to swell. Start by removing any dead, diseased, or weak canes, cutting them down to the bud union. Then, remove canes that are growing into the center of the plant. Next, select three or four of the newest and healthiest canes, and remove all of the rest. Cut the remaining canes down to 12 to 18 inches for hybrid teas and 18 to 24 inches for floribundas and grandifloras. Cut miniatures to half their former height.

Climbers should be pruned in early summer after they bloom, or you will be cutting away the flower buds. Any old, nonproductive canes should be cut to the ground, and the plant shaped. Pruning as soon as flowers fade often encourages climbers to rebloom. Dead, diseased, and damaged branches can be removed any time. Train new canes as they grow onto a fence, arbor, trellis, or other support; climbers flower more profusely if trained horizontally.

Old garden, species, shrub, and polyantha roses primarily need shaping, size control, and removal of unwanted canes, but require little other pruning.

Use common sense when pruning. If a plant appears to need pruning, you usually should go ahead and prune it, instead of strictly following the rules and waiting six to nine months later. In fact, gardeners in Zones 9 through 11 who have water shortages should forget the calendar altogether, and do their pruning at the beginning of the rainy season.

A few other gardening techniques relate to pruning. Pinching, for example, is the act of removing the growing tip of a plant with your fingers or shears. This temporarily stops top growth and encourages side growth and bushier plants. You can pinch a plant any time it needs it. Disbudding is the removal of side flower buds to encourage the central flower bud to be larger. Side buds should be disbudded as soon as they appear. Growth buds also can be disbudded, a technique useful in topiary, bonsai, and other specialized pruning techniques. Dead-heading is the removal of faded flowers, and should be done as soon as possible to encourage continued blooming.

30

HARDINESS

Hardiness refers to a plant's ability to survive within the climatic conditions it's growing in. Hardiness usually refers to the minimum winter temperature that a plant will withstand, but includes other factors as well, such as moisture, wind, soil, length of the growing season, and summer temperatures.

The United States Department of Agriculture has developed a hardiness zone map, which can be found on page 189, that divides the United States and Canada into 11 growing zones based on minimum winter temperature. Zone 1 is the coldest, with winter temperatures of –50°F or below; Zone 11 is the warmest, with minimum winter temperatures above 40°F.

Within this and other books, you'll find hardiness ratings for perennials and woody plants. These are commonly expressed as a range, because some plants need a minimum winter temperatures for dormancy or to form growth or flower buds. There-

fore, if you live in Zone 10, you will find that there are certain plants that you cannot grow, not because it gets too cold in winter, but because it doesn't get cold enough.

The lines on the zone map and the temperatures quoted are averages. In any given year, it might be colder or warmer, and plants will react accordingly.

In addition, every climate has microclimates that differ from the surrounding area. Tall buildings and fences can trap heat, warming a garden. It is also warmer on a southern slope than a northern one, or where heat reflects off pavement. It is cooler at the bottom of a hill than it is in the middle of it. If you have a microclimate in your garden, you will need to adjust your plant selection as if you gardened in a warmer or colder zone.

Hardiness affects plants in other ways, too. You might be able to grow a plant in a warmer climate than recommended if you give it more shade. A plant

that is a shrub in a cool climate could be a tree where it is warmer. A shrub that is deciduous in the North might be evergreen in the South. Spring comes earlier in warmer zones, and you may have to adjust your gardening calendar accordingly.

Annual flowers and vegetables don't depend on the zone map; their success, instead, depends on the last spring and first autumn frost dates and the summer temperatures. Read the information about planting in part one, as well as the sections on annuals and vegetables in part two, to see how to adjust your planting schedule to the plant you are growing. Keep in mind, however, that summer temperatures also can affect what can be grown. It is possible to be able to grow an annual such as lobelia in one part of Zone 9, for example, and not be able to grow it in another part, because the daytime (and more importantly, nighttime) temperatures vary during the summer.

31

WINTER PROTECTION

In any section of the country where frost occurs, you'll likely need some sort of winter protection. If you are growing a plant that is near its hardiness limit, winter protection is advised in case temperatures drop lower than normal. Plants grown at or below their hardiness limits should always be protected.

It is not always cold temperatures that cause winter damage, but alternate freezing and thawing, which heaves plants from the ground, breaking their roots and exposing them to sun, wind, and cold. A protective layer placed around a plant will reduce this effect.

Clear plastic provides excellent frost protection for cool-season vegetables.

There are several good winter blankets. Snow is the best insulator, if you are lucky enough to get a continuous cover. If not, use oak leaves, evergreen boughs (from holiday trees), soil brought in from another part of the garden, or straw. You can buy plastic foam cones that fit over small plants, or you can wrap plants in chicken wire and fill the air space with crumpled newspaper or leaves.

Apply winter protection as soon as the ground has frozen;

putting it down too early keeps the ground too warm and invites rodents to nest over winter. Remove the cover gradually as the warm days of spring start to appear; organic covers can be removed or worked into the soil.

A few other pointers will keep the garden safe from the ravages of winter. Remove snow from small and weak-wooded plants as soon as possible. Melt ice with sand instead of salt to prevent damage to plants. If the garden is windy, a wind screen will help, as will spraying plants, especially broad-leaved evergreens, with an anti-desiccant. Strong south sun can burn, even in winter, so wrap the trunks of young trees. Most importantly, make sure the plants don't enter the winter with dry roots, so water well in late autumn if it hasn't rained.

If plants have been winter damaged, prune them only after growth starts in spring; otherwise, pruning can encourage early growth that will not be able to survive late-spring frosts.

PROPAGATION

Although purchasing plants is the quickest and easiest route to landscaping your property, many gardeners prefer to propagate their own plants. New varieties of annual flowers and vegetables are available, and starting them from seeds yourself may be the only way to obtain them. In addition, as perennials, ground covers, and bulbs outgrow their spaces, they need to be divided, and this becomes an excellent way to increase your own stock or share these plants with neighbors and friends. Propagating your own plants also has economic appeal.

There are a few basic supplies you will need to propagate your own plants. First, although some plants can be started outdoors in the ground, more often than not they are started in a container, frequently indoors. You can purchase containers made of plastic, metal, compressed peat, or plastic foam. One handy container is made of compressed peat encased in mesh. When you first use it, it expands with water, and at planting time, the whole thing, plant and container, go into the ground. You also can make your own containers out of milk cartons, aluminum baking trays, plastic cooking dishes, and the like.

No matter what material you choose, there are a few important characteristics that a container should have: It should be 3 to $3^{1/2}$ inches deep for seeds and at least that deep or deeper for cuttings; it must have drainage holes in the bottom; and it must be clean. If the container is not new, wash it well with soap and water and rinse it in a solution that is 90 percent water and 10 percent household bleach. Don't ever reuse a container made of peat; you can never get it clean, and diseases can be deadly to young plants.

The same propagating medium can be used whether you are starting seeds or rooting cuttings. It should be soil-free (soil contains too many insects and diseases and is less than ideal for drainage and aeration) and fresh, never having been used before for propagating or growing. A good medium is half sphagnum peat moss and half perlite or vermiculite; you can buy this ready-made or mix it yourself. Before you place the medium into the container, moisten it first, and always pre-moisten containers made of peat. The container should be filled to within $1/4$ inch of its top.

A naturalistic perennial garden can be a joy to grow—starting with purchased plants, seeds, cuttings, offsets, or divisions.

33

Seeds grown indoors should be labeled and dated.

Peas should be direct-sown in rows outdoors.

STARTING SEEDS INDOORS

Some seeds can be sown directly in the ground outdoors, but others need a head start indoors, because either the seeds are too small to be sown outside or because the growing season isn't long enough to allow plants to grow to maturity. In the sections on annuals and vegetables that appear in part two, you'll find the requirements for starting seeds outdoors or indoors.

Timing is very important; seeds started too soon will be leggy when it comes time to plant them outdoors, while seeds started too late will not be large enough to transplant into the garden at the right time. The chapters on annuals and vegetables outline outdoor planting times; once that is determined, you can count backward to see when to sow the seeds indoors.

Most annual flowers should be started indoors six to eight weeks before outdoor planting. Calendula, celosia, marigolds, and zinnias need only four to six weeks, while begonias, coleus, geraniums, impatiens, lobelia, petunias, salvia, and snapdragons should be started 10 to 12 weeks

ahead. Most vegetables need a 5- to 7-week head start; asparagus, celery, and leeks need 10 to 12 weeks.

Biennials can be sown in summer or autumn, planted out in autumn for spring bloom, or started indoors in late winter and planted out for spring bloom the same year. Perennials can be started almost any time, depending on when you want to add them to the garden. Some perennials, as well as woody plants, need cold temperatures (stratification) to break their dormancy before they will germinate. These can be started outdoors in autumn so nature can provide the cold or placed in moist sphagnum peat moss in the refrigerator for six weeks before sowing.

Assemble your filled containers and seeds. Fine seeds can be scattered over the surface; others should be sown in rows. Cover the seeds with an amount of medium equal to their thickness and press them in lightly. Cover the container with clear plastic, and place it in good, indirect light; also provide bottom heat. Once the seeds germinate, remove the plastic and place the seeds in sun or under grow lights.

Water as needed. When the seedlings have developed two sets of true leaves, transplant them into individual pots. Ten days before outdoor planting time, get the plants used to their new environment by placing them outdoors for increasing lengths of time every day; this process is known as hardening off. Reread the earlier planting hints.

STARTING SEEDS OUTDOORS

Many seeds can be sown directly into the ground outdoors; you'll find specific plant-by-plant information in the individual chapters. The time to sow seeds outdoors generally is the same as when you would set the plants outside, especially with annual flowers, vegetables, and herbs. Perennials can be sown any time from midspring through midsummer; sow woody plants as seeds become available from midsummer through autumn. Many of these seeds will not germinate until the following spring.

Before sowing, prepare the soil, and rake it level. Make a depression in the soil, place the seeds within it, and cover with soil. Water with a fine mist every day until the seeds germinate and are growing well.

STEM CUTTINGS

Plants, particularly some annuals, some perennials, and woody plants, can be propagated from softwood or hardwood stem cuttings. Softwood cuttings are taken when plants are in growth, usually just after the plant flowered. Cut a piece of stem 4 to 6 inches long that has at least four leaves on it. Remove the bottom two leaves and all flowers and flower buds, and place the cutting in a container of propagating medium up to the bottom of the remain-

ing leaves. Most cuttings will root better if the bottom is dipped in a rooting hormone. Place a plastic bag over the container and set the container in good light but not full sun. In a few weeks, lightly

Stem cuttings should be rooted in a container with premoistened soil-less medium; a mixture of vermiculite and sphagnum peat moss is ideal.

35

Chrysanthemums are good candidates for propagation by division.

DIVISION

Many perennials and bulbs need regular dividing to prevent them from getting overcrowded and to keep them at their flowering peak. This can be done in spring when growth starts or in early autumn; it is easier to divide bulbs in spring as the foliage starts to fade because it is easier to find them then. With a spade or spading fork, gently lift the root clump from the ground and after washing the soil off, pull it apart into two or three sections. Replant immediately; share divisions you can't use with other gardeners.

There are a few other methods of propagation useful for some plants. Some perennial succulents can be propagated from leaf cuttings, and some perennials and tuberous plants can be increased by root cuttings. Woody plants with long, pliable stems can be increased by ground layering; a section of the stem is secured underground in spring or summer where it will root. When it starts to grow, perhaps the next year, it can be cut away from the mother plant and transplanted. Some plants produce offshoots, which can be cut away from the main plant, while others send out runners that produce new plants at their ends.

tug the cuttings to see if they have rooted. If they have, gradually remove the plastic bag and move the container into the sun. Once they start to grow, transplant them into individual pots until they are large enough to move to the garden.

Hardwood cuttings of woody plants are taken in autumn and placed in the ground or in a cold frame outdoors to spend the winter. They will root and start to grow the following spring.

36

INSECT AND DISEASE CONTROL

Unfortunately, insects and diseases can damage or even destroy a garden, so controlling them is essential. Always keep a sharp eye on the garden. Many insects are large enough to be seen; if not, their damage is. As soon as you spot an insect invasion, do something about it. The major insects that pester the garden are aphids, beetles, borers, caterpillars, leafhoppers, leaf miners, nematodes, scales, slugs and snails, spider mites, thrips, and whiteflies. If you don't know how to recognize these insects or

Powdery mildew is a common threat to squash plants.

the damage they may cause, ask at your garden center or nursery, or contact your county extension agent. Treatment is a top priority!

Insecticides are either contact, which when sprayed on an insect kills it, or systemic, which is absorbed by the plant and kills the insect as it feeds. Insecticides can also be organic or inorganic; which you choose is a matter of personal choice, although some insects dictate the choice. Scales, for example, require a systemic insecticide since their hard outer layers make contact insecticides just about useless. Some insecticides, such as soap and dormant oil, smother insects and their eggs without harming birds and pets.

Diseases often are harder to diagnose than insects. The main diseases that plague gardens are anthracnose, aster yellows, botrytis blight, canker, crown gall, damping off, fire blight, leaf spot, mildew, mosaic, root rot, rust, and scab. If you are not sure what is plaguing your garden, ask at the garden center or nursery,

or contact your county extension agent. They can recommend a fungicide to correct the problem.

Diseases often are difficult to cure, so the most effective things you can do to prevent their spread to other garden plants are to spray, prune away diseased plant parts, or even remove the plant itself. The spread of diseases is also kept to a minimum by using mulch, watering plants only in the morning, cleaning up gardening debris, rotating plants, increasing air circulation, controlling insects, and keeping the garden weed-free, which also reduces insect populations. These gardening tasks are continuous, but worth the effort.

Insecticides and fungicides can be applied in dust form but usually are applied in liquid form with a sprayer. These come in several different types, depending on your budget and your needs. Spray well-watered plants on a calm day, making sure both sides of the leaves are covered with spray. Spray whenever it is necessary—if you put it off, you'll be sorry.

37

PLANNING THE GARDEN

Why do we garden? Perhaps because it is relaxing or because it takes us outdoors, close to nature. For most gardeners, however, the appeal lies in creating pleasant surroundings to complement a home and afford an outdoor living room.

Planning a garden brings with it the joy of anticipation and is best carried out in advance rather than helter-skelter. There are many things to consider when planning a garden. Of crucial importance is to match the plants you'd like to grow to your environment. First, take into account the available light. Is the garden in full sun (six hours or more a day), light shade (dappled sunlight), part shade (four to six hours of sun a day), or shade (less than four hours of sun a day)? Second, analyze your soil, and determine your watering needs and availability. Third, consider temperature. Is the garden cool (under 70°F in summer), average (70° to 85°F), or hot (more than

38

Formal gardens incorporate straight lines and geometric patterns, and very often contain carefully clipped hedges and shrubs.

85°F)? Keep in mind that a garden that is hot during the day but cool at night may still be able to support cool-weather plants, opening your doors to a larger selection of plants. You'll also need to consider plant hardiness.

Once you have analyzed your environment, you can then choose plants that will thrive— and that you need or would like to grow. You may want trees to frame the yard or provide shade, shrubs to hide the foundation or act as accents, hedges to divide one section of the garden from another or your yard from your neighbor's, vines to hide eyesores, a lawn to play on, vegetables and herbs for a tasty menu, or flowers for color, line, fragrance, unity, or cutting.

Plan the garden first; laying it out on graph paper is a good idea. Select a color scheme for each season, and plants with a variety of shapes and textures. You may want to enhance the garden with raised beds (which also could be a necessity in areas with poor soil or drainage), container plants, or a specialty garden such as a rock garden or water garden. Once you have mapped out your plans, you are well on your way to creating a garden you will enjoy for many years.

39

PART 2

THE PLANTS

From ground covers to flowers to trees, plants of

all shapes and sizes are presented in this section. Refer

to each plant category for helpful planting and

growing information as well as handy maintenance

tips and detailed plant listings.

ANNUALS

Often started indoors from seed, verbena is a sun-loving annual.

By definition, an annual is a plant that grows, flowers, sets seed, and dies in the same growing season. Some plants that are perennial in frost-free climates, such as vinca and impatiens, can be grown as annuals in colder climates because they come into flower quickly. Some biennials, too, can be grown as annuals if they are started early enough in the season.

Well loved for providing splashes of color and finishing touches to the garden, annuals have an instant effect on the landscape. Because their blooming period is so long, they bring a continuity of color unmatched by most other flowering plants. Available in a wide variety of colors, shapes, and sizes, annuals can unite sections of a garden, be used as accents or foils, or be planted into traditional beds and borders. And because they are temporary plants, it is possible to experiment with different color themes: Go "cool" one season by planting various shades of blue and "hot" the next with reds and oranges.

Annuals are divided into two categories. Those known as cool-season annuals prefer growing temperatures under 70°F and are grown in spring and autumn or during the summer in places where the temperature does not soar. Warm-season annuals need warm to hot temperatures to grow and are added to the garden after all danger of frost has passed. Pay attention to night temperatures as well as daytime temperatures when selecting annuals; some cool-weather annuals will thrive even when the days are hot if nights are cool.

Annuals also are categorized as very hardy, hardy, half-hardy, or tender. Very hardy plants tolerate heavy frost, while hardy plants can withstand light frost. Half-hardy plants grow well in cool temperatures but will not tolerate frost, and tender annuals need not only frost-free weather but also warm temperatures.

The first step in selecting annuals for your garden is to match a list of plants to your climate. Next, narrow the list to those that match your light, soil, and water conditions. These factors are outlined in the plant listings that follow. Once this is

done, choose those with the size, shape, or flower color that will most enhance your garden and that you find most pleasing.

Annuals have uses almost everywhere in the garden. Traditional beds can break up an expanse of lawn, while borders can line walkways, driveways, and fences. An evergreen foundation planting can come alive with colorful summer annuals, and beds can add interest to trees or mailboxes. Low-growing annuals can be used as ground covers or in rock gardens, while climbing types can cover trellises, fences, and arbors, creating a wall of color, providing shade, or hiding an eyesore. Many annuals also add a delicious fragrance to outdoor areas.

As accents, annuals grow well in containers or hanging baskets, while many can be chosen to use their flowers for cutting and drying. They can be planted in mass, using either one or several varieties of the same type of plant, or they can be grown in mixed beds and borders. The decision is up to you, but simpler designs usually have better visual effects. In addition, don't think of annuals as plants that can only stand alone. Mix them with perennials, bulbs, or roses for an attractive mixed flower planting.

Flats of annuals (ABOVE) can be purchased at any garden center and should be kept well watered until they are added to the garden (BELOW), where they will provide a season of continuous color.

PLANTING AND GROWING ANNUALS

Although a few annuals, such as coleus, begonias, and geraniums, can be grown from cuttings, most annuals are grown from seeds. If you choose to start your own plants from seed, refer to the tips given in the section on propagation in part one. Some seeds can be sown directly into the garden, while others must have a head start indoors. These requirements are spelled out in the plant listings that follow. If you don't wish to start your own plants from seeds, bedding plants are available from many retail outlets at their specific planting times. Look for healthy, green plants and choose those (except for most African marigolds) not in bud or bloom; these will grow and flower better once planted in your own garden.

Planting time varies with each plant's hardiness and your climate. Very hardy annuals can be planted as soon as the soil can be worked in late winter or early spring. Hardy annuals are planted a little later, about four weeks before the last frost. Half-hardy and tender annuals are planted after frost danger has passed, but tender annuals

need warmer soil than half-hardy plants, so wait even a little longer to plant them. Whether you have grown your own seeds or purchased bedding plants, keep the plants well watered until planting time, and try to plant on a cloudy day or late in the afternoon, which will help the plants avoid transplanting shock (petu-

Designing a garden with a color theme is easy with annuals—and changeable from year to year.

nias are a rare exception to this rule). Refer to the timetable in part three for planting guidelines for your area.

Planting distances are outlined in the plant listings that follow. When planting into hanging baskets, containers, or planters, place plants closer than normally recommended so the planting will have a fuller look.

Once planted, water annuals daily until they show signs of new growth. After that, water those with average moisture requirements once a week, watering deeply to encourage deep roots. Those that need more or less moisture than average can be watered accordingly. Water early in the day to avoid diseases, and if you are growing flowers for cutting, avoid overhead watering if possible.

Except for cosmos, moss roses, nasturtiums, spider flowers, and treasure flowers, which prefer infertile soil, annuals grow best in rich soil and should be well fed. Incorporate a balanced fertilizer, such as 5-10-5, into the soil before planting, and fertilize once or twice more during the growing season or more often if the plants are not growing well.

Annuals that tend to become leggy, such as pansies, petunias,

and snapdragons, will benefit from pinching out the growing tip at planting time or after the first flush of bloom. Any other annual that becomes leggy can be treated this way as well. As soon as the flowers of any annual have faded (with the exception of ageratum, begonias, coleus, impatiens, lobelia, sweet alyssum, and vinca, whose flowers fall off cleanly), cut off the dead flowers to encourage new growth and flowering. If you cut flowers for creating arrangements, you will be doing this automatically. Annuals that sprawl, such as candytuft, lobelia, phlox, sweet alyssum, and some types of vinca, can be kept in bounds by heading them back with hedge clippers or scissors.

Keep annual beds and borders weed-free, and mulch them to keep down weeds and conserve soil moisture. Tall or weak-stemmed annuals may need to be staked and tied to prevent them from falling over. As with any plant, keep an eye out for signs of insects and diseases, and treat plants immediately if there is a problem. Refer to the timetable in part three for recommendations as to when to plant and perform routine maintenance chores in your area.

45

A GARDENER'S LIST OF ANNUALS

AGERATUM

Below is an alphabetical list by botanical name of the most popular annuals. Under each listing is a description of the plant's growth and flowering, plus the light, soil, and climatic requirements (which are fully explained earlier in this section). Also refer to the Average Frost Date Maps on page 188.

AGERATUM HOUSTONIANUM
(Ageratum)

Fluffy flowers of primarily blue but sometimes pink or white smother 4- to 8-inch plants. Start these half-hardy plants indoors and space 5 to 7 inches apart. Sun or part shade; average to moist soil; average temperatures.

ANTIRRHINUM MAJUS
(Snapdragon)

Blooms in a rainbow of colors cover spikes on 6- to 30-inch plants. Very hardy; plants can be grown from seeds started indoors or outdoors. Space 6 to 12 inches apart. Sun; average to moist soil; cool to average temperatures.

BEGONIA X SEMPER-FLORENS-CULTORUM
(Begonia)

Generally called wax begonias to distinguish them from tuberous types, begonias have small flowers of white, pink, or red on mounded 6- to 8-inch plants. These half-hardy plants should be started indoors (it's hard to produce good plants from seed, however; most gardeners plant purchased transplants) and spaced 7 to 9 inches apart. Part shade to shade; average soil and temperatures.

BRASSICA OLERACEA
(Flowering kale or cabbage)

Grown for their colorful pink, white, or purplish foliage, primarily in autumn or winter's cool weather, plants grow 15 to 18 inches high. Start plants indoors and plant 15 to 18 inches apart. Very hardy; sun; moist soil.

46

CALENDULA OFFICINALIS

(Pot marigold)

Edible and perky daisylike flowers of orange or yellow bloom atop hardy 10- to 20-inch plants. Start indoors or outdoors and space 8 to 10 inches apart. Sun or light shade; moist soil; cool to average climate.

CALLISTEPHUS CHINENSIS

(China aster)

Mixed-colored, daisylike flowers bloom on 6- to 30-inch plants. Start seeds indoors or outdoors and space plants 6 to 18 inches apart. Watch for aster yellows disease, and rotate planting sites every year. Half-hardy; sun or part shade; moist soil; average temperatures.

CAPSICUM ANNUUM

(Ornamental pepper)

These 4- to 8-inch plants are grown for their tiny round or tapered yellow, red, or orange edible (but fiery hot) peppers. Half-hardy plants should be started indoors and spaced 5 to 7 inches apart. Sun or part shade; moist soil; average to hot temperatures.

CATHARANTHUS ROSEUS

(Vinca)

Also called periwinkle, spreading or upright half-hardy plants are 4 to 12 inches tall and topped with white, pink, or rose-colored flowers. Start seeds indoors (outdoors in frost-free climates) and space 6 to 8 inches apart. Sun or light shade; any soil; average to hot temperatures.

CENTAUREA CINERARIA

(Dusty-miller)

Grown for its white, gray, or silver foliage, dusty-miller grows 8 to 10 inches tall. Start seeds indoors and space 6 to 8 inches apart. Sun to part shade; dry to average soil; average to hot climate.

CELOSIA CRISTATA

(Cockscomb)

Flowers in bright, mixed colors are either featherlike or rippled on 6- to 20-inch half-hardy plants. Start seeds indoors or outside, but don't plant too early. Space 6 to 10 inches apart. Sun; dry soil; average to hot temperatures.

CLEOME HASSLERANA

(Spider flower)

Spiderlike flowers are pink or white on 30- to 48-inch half-hardy plants. Start seeds indoors or outdoors and space 12 to 15 inches apart. Sun; dry soil; average to hot climate.

COLEUS X HYBRIDUS

(Coleus)

Grown for their brightly colored and patterned foliage, coleus has insignificant spikes of blue flow-

COSMOS

ers. Tender plants grow 10 to 24 inches tall. Start seeds or cuttings indoors and space 8 to 10 inches apart. Part shade to shade; average to moist soil; average to hot temperatures.

COSMOS SPECIES

(Cosmos)

Daisylike flowers have mixed colors and bloom atop 18- to 30-inch plants. Start seeds indoors or outdoors and plant 9 to 18 inches apart. Half-hardy; sun; dry to average soil; average temperatures.

COCKSCOMB

GAILLARDIA PULCHELLA

(Blanket flower)

Daisylike flowers of red and orange bloom on 10- to 18-inch half-hardy plants. Seeds can be started indoors or outdoors; space plants 8 to 15 inches apart. Sun or light shade; dry to average soil; average to hot climate.

GAZANIA RIGENS

(Treasure flower)

Gold, yellow, or orange flowers bloom atop 6- to 10-inch half-hardy plants. Start seeds inside or outside and space plants 8 to 10 inches apart. Sun; dry to average soil; average to hot climate.

HELIANTHUS ANNUUS

(Sunflower)

Huge yellow flowers top 15-inch to 12-foot plants. Start seeds indoors or outdoors and space 12 to 24 inches apart. Sun; dry soil; hot weather.

IBERIS SPECIES

(Candytuft)

Upright or spreading half-hardy plants grow 8 to 10 inches high and have white, pink, or lavender blooms. Start seeds indoors or outside and space 7 to 9 inches apart. Sun; dry to average soil; any climate.

IMPATIENS WALLERANA

(Impatiens)

Flowers in almost any color smother tender 6- to 18-inch plants. Start seeds indoors and space 8 to 10 inches apart. Part shade to shade; average soil and temperatures.

IPOMOEA SPECIES

(Morning-glory)

Upright or vining plants grow 5 inches to 6 feet tall and have flowers in mixed colors. Start seeds inside or outside and space tender plants 12 to 18 inches apart. Sun; moist soil; average climate.

LATHYRUS ODORATUS

(Sweet pea)

Upright or vining hardy plants grow 2 inches to 5 feet tall and have fragrant flowers in mixed colors. Sow seeds outdoors and space 6 to 15 inches apart. Sun; moist soil; cool to average climate.

LOBELIA ERINUS

(Lobelia)

Bright blue or purple blooms cover 3- to 5-inch spreading, half-hardy plants. Start seeds indoors and space 8 to 10 inches apart. Sun in cool areas, otherwise part shade; moist soil; cool to average climate.

LOBULARIA MARITIMA

(Sweet alyssum)

White, pink, or lavender fragrant flowers cover 3- to 6-inch spreading hardy plants. Start seeds indoors or outdoors and space 10 to 12 inches apart. Sun to part shade; average to moist soil; average to hot climate.

NICOTIANA ALATA

(Flowering tobacco)

Funnel-shaped blooms in mixed colors flower on 12- to 15-inch half-hardy plants. Seeds are started inside or outside and plants are spaced 8 to 10 inches apart. Sun to part shade; moist soil; average to hot temperatures.

PELARGONIUM X HORTORUM

(Geranium)

Globular blooms in mixed colors flower on 10- to 15-inch plants. Start seeds or cuttings indoors and space tender plants 10 to 12 inches apart. Sun; average to moist soil; average temperatures.

PETUNIA X HYBRIDA

(Petunia)

Spreading 6- to 12-inch half-hardy plants have trumpetlike blooms in a variety of colors. Start seeds indoors and space 10 to 12 inches apart. Sun; dry soil; average to hot weather.

48

IMPATIENS

LOBELIA

GERANIUMS

SWEET ALYSSUM

PHLOX DRUMMONDII

(Phlox)

Blooms in mixed colors flower on 6- to 10-inch plants. Start seeds inside or outside and space 7 to 9 inches apart. Sun; moist soil; cool to average temperatures.

SALVIA SPLENDENS

(Salvia)

Also called scarlet sage, half-hardy plants have red, white, or purple spiked flowers. Start seeds indoors and space 6 to 8 inches apart. Sun to part shade; average to moist soil; average to hot temperatures.

PETUNIAS

PORTULACA GRANDIFLORA

(Moss rose)

Blooms in a rainbow of colors flower on 4- to 6-inch tender, spreading plants, usually when the sun shines. Start seeds indoors or outdoors and space 6 to 8 inches apart. Sun; well-drained soil; hot weather.

TAGETES ERECTA

(African marigold)

Gold, yellow, or orange flowers bloom on 18- to 30-inch half-hardy plants. Most need to be in bud or bloom at planting time to flower all summer. Start seeds indoors and space 12 to 15 inches apart. Sun; average soil and temperatures.

49

TAGETES PATULA

(French marigold)

Gold or yellow blooms top 5- to 10-inch half-hardy plants. Start seeds indoors or outdoors and space 3 to 6 inches apart. Sun; average soil and temperatures.

VERBENA X HYBRIDA

(Verbena)

Mixed colors appear on 6- to 8-inch plants. Start seeds indoors and plant 5 to 7 inches apart. Sun; dry to average soil; hot weather.

VIOLA X WITTROCKIANA

(Pansy)

Flowers of mixed colors bloom on 4- to 8-inch very hardy plants. Start seeds indoors and plant 6 to 8 inches apart. Sun to part shade; moist soil; cool temperatures.

PANSIES

TROPAEOLUM MAJUS

(Nasturtium)

Blooms of yellow, orange, or red appear on spreading or upright 12- to 24-inch plants. Start seeds outdoors and thin to 8 to 12 inches apart. Sun to light shade; dry soil; cool to average climate.

ZINNIA ELEGANS

(Zinnia)

Tender 4-inch to 3-foot plants with flowers in a rainbow of colors. Start seeds inside or outside and space 4 to 24 inches apart. Sun; dry to average soil; average to—better yet—hot weather.

50

PERENNIALS AND BIENNIALS

Whereas annuals can be considered accessories in the garden design, perennials and biennials can be regarded as the basic wardrobe. Perennials are plants that grow and flower each year (even though the blooming period may last only four to six weeks), then go dormant during the winter, usually dying to the ground (although a few remain evergreen, especially in warm climates). Because perennials are available in such a range of plant sizes, flower colors, and blooming times, they can be included in the garden to give dependable and almost continuous color from early spring until late autumn.

A biennial is a plant that requires two growing seasons to grow and flower. Growth takes place in the first season, and then, after overwintering, the plant blooms and dies. Biennials often can be grown as annuals if given an early start indoors; some, such as foxglove and money plant, reseed themselves so easily that they act in effect as perennials.

Think beyond flower color and shape when selecting perennials; look also for a wide variety of foliage textures and colors that will add interest to the garden once the flowers have faded.

51

Perennials have a vast array of uses in the garden. Large-growing plants, such as peonies, can stand alone as specimens. They can accent a corner of a patio or break up a large expanse of lawn. Some perennials can be planted by themselves, while others can be mixed together in flower beds or borders, usually looking best if grouped into at least threes. Ground-hugging types can border walkways, driveways, or foundation plantings. As ground covers, they can unite different sections of the garden. Although perennials usually are not grown in containers, those with long blooming periods will fit this bill nicely.

Biennials have a short blooming period, usually in spring to early summer, so they are good to use as seasonal accents. Mix them freely with other flowering plants, or grow them on their own. They can be considered temporary plants, to be replaced with annuals when their blooming period is finished.

Delphiniums can be grown from seed, provided the seeds are fresh and have not been stored. Once planted, keep the roots of these spiky blue-flowering plants moist and cool.

Many perennials and biennials have a delicious fragrance, so place them where you can enjoy their scent. Many perennials and biennials are excellent as cut flowers, and low-growing plants of either type are excellent in rock gardens.

If your home is formal in style, you can embellish it with a formal garden design. Informal

homes look better with an informal, or "country" or "cottage," type of mixed planting. Just be careful that the overall effect is not spotty. Perennials and bienni-als need not stand alone; they can be combined with annuals, bulbs, or roses so your beds or borders always have color.

When selecting perennials and biennials for the garden, consider several factors. Tall plants can be chosen for the back of a border or against walls or fences. Medium-size plants fit into the middle of the bed or border, while low-growing types can be used as edgings or ground covers. Next select a color scheme, which can be different for each season, and choose plants that fit that scheme.

For longer color, pick plants with different blooming periods. Select a combination of tall, spiky plants and lower-growing, rounded ones for visual appeal. Perennials and biennials also have different foliage textures, and a combination of delicate and coarse leaves is attractive, especially when the plants are not in bloom. Match the plants to your growing conditions of light, soil, and temperature, which are outlined in the plant listing that follows. Also check the plants' hardiness, making sure they will survive winters in your area, and keeping in mind that some perennials require cold winters to grow and bloom.

PLANTING AND GROWING PERENNIALS AND BIENNIALS

Perennials can be added to the garden in a variety of ways. You can purchase plants from retail stores or from mail-order nurs-eries, which often sell bare-root plants, or start your own from seeds, cuttings, offsets, or divi-sions. Gardening friends often have extras to spare and share. Biennials can be purchased, or you may be able to get seedlings from friends. Otherwise, they usually are grown from seed. Started indoors in late winter or early spring, they may bloom the first year; started in summer and overwintered, they will bloom the following year. The ways of propagating perennials and bien-nials are outlined in the plant listing that follows, and how-to instructions are given in the propagation section of part one.

Almost without exception, perennials and biennials prefer rich, fertile, well-drained, neutral soil, which you can read about in part one. Because perennials are permanent plants, it is important that the soil be well prepared. Planting or transplanting of

53

perennials can be done in early spring when growth starts or in early autumn. The major exceptions are poppies, irises, and peonies, which must be transplanted in autumn so their blooming cycle isn't interrupted. Biennials started so they bloom the first year should be planted in early spring; otherwise, plant them between midsummer and six weeks before the first autumn frost.

Perennials and biennials planted the previous year should be fed with a balanced fertilizer in spring when growth starts. Most won't need additional feeding, but if they are not growing strongly, fertilize them again after they bloom. Plants with average water requirements should receive 1 inch of water per week; for those with higher or lower moisture requirements, adjust watering as needed. Water deeply and infrequently to encourage strong, deep-growing roots.

As soon as flowers have faded, remove them. This will encourage new growth and, in some cases, repeat flowering. If you snip cut flowers for indoor use or for drying, you automatically will be grooming the plants. The main exception to this rule is if you want the plants to reseed, as is the case with some biennials; then you should leave the flowers or seeds on the plant so they can fall freely to the ground. Low-growing plants can be sheared back with hedge clippers after flowering to keep the plants neat. Plants that grow tall and lanky, like chrysanthemums, will benefit from having their growing tips removed early in the season to encourage bushiness. If you want large, showcase flowers on such plants as peonies, remove all side flower buds as they appear.

Daylily flowers last for only one day, but their blooming period continues for many weeks.

54

Keep flower beds weed-free; a mulch will help accomplish this as well as conserve soil moisture. Keep an eye out for insects and diseases and treat if needed; perennials prone to mildew, such as phlox, should not be watered overhead, if at all possible, to keep the leaves dry. Tall perennials and biennials often need to be staked or tied.

When perennials become crowded, when blooming slows down or ceases, or if the centers of the plants die out, it is time to dig them up, divide, and replant them. Except for those perennials that must be planted in autumn, this can be done in spring when growth starts or in autumn. As a general rule, divide and transplant summer- and autumn-flowering plants in spring, and spring-flowering plants the previous autumn.

In late autumn or winter, after frost has blackened the tops of perennials, cut them almost to the ground, leaving about $1/2$ inch of stems so you will know where they are next spring. Cutting them down not only is more attractive, it also lessens breeding spots for insects and diseases over winter. Remove and store all stakes at this time as well.

As soon as a hard frost hits and you've cut back the tops of your perennials, apply winter protection if necessary. This will help keep the plants alive and prevent frost from heaving small plants from the ground.

Many wildflowers are perennials and are grown in much the same way, except that wildflowers by their nature do not require much intervention. If grown in a meadow, mow in autumn after the flowers have faded.

Coralbells are easily propagated by division.

55

A GARDENER'S LIST OF PERENNIALS AND BIENNIALS

ASTERS

The list below outlines the most popular perennials and biennials, listed in alphabetical order by their botanical name. Besides a description of the plant and its flowers, the list details each plant's blooming period, climatic requirements, method of propagation, and hardiness zone (see the map on page 189).

ACHILLEA SPECIES

(Yarrow)

Perennial. Flat clusters of pink, white, or yellow flowers bloom on 2- to 3-foot plants in early summer and again in autumn. Plant 1 to 2 feet apart in sun, dry soil, and average to hot temperatures. Division, seeds. Zones 3–8.

ALCEA ROSEA

(Hollyhock)

Perennial or biennial. Open flowers in mixed colors appear on 4- to 10-foot spikes in early summer. May freely reseed. Set 1½ feet apart in sun, moist soil, and average temperatures. Seeds. Zones 3–8.

AQUILEGIA SPECIES

(Columbine)

Perennial. Unique drooping flowers in mixed colors, often two-toned, bloom on 1- to 3-foot plants in late spring. Plant 1½ feet apart in sun or light shade, average to moist soil, and

cool to average temperatures. Seeds, division. Zones 3–8.

ASTER SPECIES

(Aster)

Perennial. Daisylike flowers in mixed colors, but most often blue or purple, bloom in late summer and autumn on 2- to 8-foot plants. Set 1 to 3 feet apart in sun, average soil, and average temperatures. Seeds, division. Zones 3–9.

ASTILBE SPECIES

(Astilbe)

Perennial. Spikes of fluffy white, pink, or red flowers bloom on 1- to 3-foot plants in early summer. Makes a good cut or dried flower. Plant 1 to 3 feet apart in light shade, average to moist soil, and average climate. Division. Zones 4–8.

AURINIA SAXATILIS

(Basket-of-gold)

Perennial. Also called alyssum. Clusters of golden flowers appear on 6- to 12-inch plants in early to midspring. Plant 1 foot apart in sun, moist soil, and cool to average temperatures. Seeds. Zones 4–10.

BELLIS PERENNIS

(English daisy)

Biennial. Small daisy-shaped flowers of white, pink, or red bloom in late summer or early spring on 6-inch plants. Space 6 inches apart in sun or part shade, moist soil, and cool temperatures. Seeds. Zones 3–7.

CAMPANULA SPECIES

(Bellflower)

Perennial or biennial. Bell-shaped flowers of blue or white bloom on plants 6 inches to 5 feet high from late spring to midsummer, depending on the species. Space 6 inches to 2 feet apart in sun or light shade, average to moist soil, and average temperatures. Division, seeds. Zones 3–9.

CHELONE LYONII

(Turtlehead)

Perennial. Deep pink flowers appear on 3- to 4-foot spikes in late summer and autumn. Give them sun or light shade, moist soil, and average temperatures, and plant 2 feet apart. Seeds, cuttings. Zones 4–9.

CHRYSANTHEMUM SPECIES

(Chrysanthemum)

Perennial. The flower synonymous with autumn has a vast variety of flower colors and shapes. Plants grow 6 inches to 5 feet tall and should be spaced 6 inches to 2 feet apart. Older types need long nights to bloom; newer varieties are less light sensitive. Sun, average to moist soil, average temperatures. Seeds, cuttings, division. Zones 3–11.

COREOPSIS SPECIES

(Tickseed)

Perennial. Daisylike yellow flowers bloom on $1^{1/2}$- to 3-foot plants from early to late summer, making this one of the longest-blooming perennials. Some have very fine foliage. Plant 1 to $1^{1/2}$ feet apart in sun, average to moist soil, average to hot climate. Seeds, division. Zones 4–11.

DELPHINIUM SPECIES

(Delphinium)

Perennial. Spikes of blue, purple, or white flowers appear on 1- to 6-foot plants in early summer. Keep the roots moist and cool; plants also like sun and cool weather. Seeds, division. Zones 3–10.

DIANTHUS BARBATUS

(Sweet William)

Biennial. Clusters of flat, fragrant flowers of primarily pink or red bloom on 6-inch to 2-foot plants in late spring or early summer. Space 6 to 9 inches apart in sun, average to moist soil, and cool to average temperatures. Seeds. Zones 3–7.

DICENTRA SPECIES

(Bleeding-heart)

Perennial. Deep pink to red, drooping, heart-shaped flowers appear on arching branches in midspring. The foliage of *D. spectabilis* may disappear in midsummer; *D. exima* remains green all summer. Plants are 2 to 3 feet tall and should be planted $1^{1/2}$ to 2 feet apart. Part shade, moist soil, average temperatures. Seeds, division. Zones 3–9.

HOLLYHOCKS

BELLFLOWERS

BLEEDING-HEART

FOXGLOVE

GLOBE THISTLE

DAYLILY

DIGITALIS PURPUREA

(Foxglove)

Biennial. Drooping flowers in mixed colors appear on 1- to 3-foot spikes in late spring to early summer. Plant 15 to 24 inches apart in sun or part shade, average to moist soil, and average temperatures. Seeds. Zones 4–7.

ECHINACEA PURPUREA

(Purple coneflower)

Perennial. Daisylike purple flowers with drooping petals bloom in midsummer on 2- to 4-foot plants. Plant 2 feet apart in sun or light shade, average to dry soil, and average temperatures. Division, cuttings, seeds. Zones 3–11.

ECHINOPS RITRO

(Globe thistle)

Perennial. Globular purple flowers bloom in midsummer on 2- to 4-foot plants with prickly foliage. Set 1¹/₂ to 2 feet apart in sun, dry soil, and average to hot temperatures. Division. Zones 3–9.

GAILLARDIA X GRANDIFLORA

(Blanket flower)

Perennial. Daisy-shaped flowers of red, yellow, and gold bloom from early to late summer, making this one of the longest blooming perennials. Plants grow 1 to 3 feet tall and should be spaced 1¹/₂ feet apart in sun, dry soil, and average to hot climate. Seeds, division. Zones 3–8.

GERANIUM SPECIES

(Cranesbill)

Perennial. Not to be confused with the annual geranium (*Pelargonium* species), this relative grows only 6 inches to 1 foot tall and has pink, red, and sometimes blue flowers in late spring. Plant 1 foot apart in sun or light shade, moist soil, and average temperatures. Seeds, division. Zones 3–11.

HEMEROCALLIS SPECIES AND HYBRIDS

(Daylily)

Perennial. One of the most reliable perennials for the garden,

daylilies have trumpet-shaped flowers in shades of white, yellow, gold, and red. Each flower lasts only one day, but the blooming period covers many weeks. With the right selection of species and varieties, daylilies can be in bloom from late spring to late summer. Set the 1- to 6-foot plants 1 to 3 feet apart in light to part shade, and average soil and climate. Division. Zones 3–10.

HEUCHERA SANGUINEA

(Coralbells)

Perennial. Tiny pink or red flowers bloom above 6- to 12-inch plants in early summer. Plant 1 foot apart in sun or light shade, moist soil, and average climate. Division. Zones 3–10.

HOSTA SPECIES AND HYBRIDS

(Plantain lily)

Perennial. This 6-inch to 3-foot plant (sometimes called funkia) is grown mostly for its foliage, which may be variegated and highly textured, but it does pro-

58

duce spikes of white or lavender flowers from mid- to late summer, depending on the variety. Often used as a ground cover. Set 1 to 3 feet apart in part shade, moist soil, and average temperatures. Division. Zones 3–9.

IBERIS SEMPERVIRENS

(Candytuft)

Perennial. Clusters of white flowers cover 12-inch spreading plants in midspring; this is a good ground cover plant. Space 1 foot apart in sun, moist soil, and cool to average temperatures. Seeds, division. Zones 4–8.

IRIS X GERMANICA

(Iris, bearded)

Perennial. This plant, which grows from a rhizome, has 1- to 4-foot spikes of flowers in mixed colors in early summer. It likes sun, dry soil, and average temperatures, and is planted 1 foot apart. Division, seeds. Zones 3–9.

LUNARIA ANNUA

(Honesty)

Biennial. Sometimes called money plant because its dried seed pods are shaped like coins. Plants grow 3 feet tall and have pink flowers in late spring or early summer. Space 1 foot apart in part shade and average soil and climate. Reseeds very easily. Seeds. Zones 3–8.

LUPINUS HYBRIDS

(Lupine)

Perennial. Dense 3- to 4-foot spikes of brightly colored flowers bloom in late spring. It likes sun but moist, cool soil and cool to average temperatures. Plant 2 feet apart. Seeds. Zones 3–9.

PAEONIA OFFICINALIS

(Peony)

Perennial. This 2- to 4-foot plant literally can be covered in large single or double fragrant flowers in shades of white, pink, or red in early summer. Space 3 feet apart with "eyes" 2 inches deep in sun and average soil and climate. May need staking. Division. Zones 3–8.

PAPAVER ORIENTALE

(Poppy)

Perennial. Also called Oriental poppy, this plant has large, brightly colored flowers primarily in shades of red, orange, yellow, and white in early summer. Plants grow 3 to 4 feet tall and are spaced 8 to 12 inches apart. Grow in sun, dry soil, and average to cool climate. The foliage will disappear in hot summers and regrow in fall. Division, cuttings, seeds. Zones 3–8.

PEONY

IRIS

HONESTY

POPPY

PHLOX PANICULATA

(Phlox)

Perennial. This workhorse of the midsummer garden has clusters of fragrant flowers in varied colors on 3- to 4-foot plants. Space 2 feet apart in sun, dry soil, and average climate. Watch for mildew. Division (grows from seed, but does not always produce desirable colors). Zones 3–10.

PHLOX STOLONIFERA

(Creeping phlox)

Perennial. This spreading plant grows 6 inches tall, making it a good ground cover, and has lavender to blue flowers in mid-spring. Plant 1 foot apart in full sun to light shade, moist soil, and average temperatures. Division. Zones 3–10.

PRIMULA SPECIES

(Primrose)

Perennial. Clusters of brightly colored flowers bloom on 6-inch to 3-foot plants in early spring. Space these naturally short-lived plants 6 inches to 1 foot apart in part shade, moist soil, and cool temperatures. Seeds, division. Zones 4–10.

RUDBECKIA HIRTA

(Black-eyed Susan)

Perennial. Once a roadside flower, improved varieties are grown in the garden for their daisylike yellow flowers that

60

PHLOX

PRIMROSES

bloom all summer. Plants grow 2
to 3 feet tall and are spaced 1 to
1 1/2 feet apart. Sun, dry soil,
average to hot climate. Seeds,
division. Zones 4–9.

SEDUM SPECIES

(Stonecrop)

Perennial. This succulent has clusters of flowers, primarily yellow
on the spring-blooming types and
pink or red on the autumn-
blooming ones. It is a good
ground cover, especially the
lower-growing types. Plants range
from 3 inches to 2 feet tall and are
planted 1 to 2 feet apart. Low-
growing types spread quickly.
Plant in sun, average to dry soil,
and average to hot temperatures.
Division, cuttings. Zones 3–11.

TRILLIUM SPECIES

(Wake-Robin)

Perennial. White or purple flowers grace this 6-inch to 1 1/2-foot
plant in midspring. Plant 1 foot
apart in part shade, moist soil,
and average to cool temperatures.
Division, seeds. Zones 3–8.

TROLLIUS EUROPAEUS

(Globeflower)

Balls of golden flowers bloom in
midspring on 1 1/2-foot plants.
Plant 1 foot apart in part shade,
moist soil, and cool to average climate. Division, seeds. Zones 5–10.

STONECROP

VERONICA SPITCATA

(Speedwell)

Perennial. Spikes of mostly blue but
sometimes white flowers appear on
1- to 3-foot plants in early to midsummer. Space 1 foot apart in sun,
moist soil, and average temperatures. Division. Zones 4–10.

VIOLA SPECIES

(Violet)

Perennial. Perky, sometimes fragrant flowers in mixed colors
resemble the pansy and bloom on
6- to 12-inch plants in midspring.
Space 6 inches apart in light to
part shade, moist soil, and cool to
average temperatures. Division,
seeds, offsets. Zones 3–10.

61

BULBS

Bulbs are one of nature's miracles. Inside a not-so-attractive package lies the potential for beautiful flowers and foliage that grow, bloom, die back, then lie dormant until the next growing season. The blooming period of many bulbs is not long, but most are permanent garden plants that reward you with color year after year.

Five categories of plants are grouped together under the term *bulb* because of their similarities in growth and food storage. True bulbs (daffodils, hyacinths, lilies, and tulips) are complete: Inside fleshy, food-storing scales are the future roots, stems, foliage, and flowers. After the bulb flowers, the leaves turn yellow as they manufacture food for the next season, transferring that food back into the bulb. Bulbs usually are covered with a papery skin.

Small bulblets, which can be removed from the mother bulb to grow into new plants, form around the base of bulbs. Some

A tuberous root, Persian buttercups (*Ranunculus asiaticus*) produce bright, papery blooms all summer.

62

bulbs, such as lilies, form bulbils where the leaf meets the stem.

Corms (crocuses, freesias, and gladiolus) are modified stems filled with food-storing cells. They usually are short and squat, covered in mesh, and have growth "eyes" at the top. After a corm blooms, it dies, but a new one forms for the following year's growth and flowers. Some corms form cormels, which are similar to bulblets.

Rhizomes (canna) are thick food-storing stems that grow on top of or just below the soil's surface. Once a rhizome has bloomed, it will not grow or flower again; a new rhizome forms to grow and flower the following season.

Tubers (caladiums, tuberous begonias) are thick food-storing stems that grow underground and have growth buds at the top. They increase in size every year and can be cut apart to form new plants.

Tuberous roots (dahlias) are thick, food-storing structures that resemble tubers but die out every year and are replaced by new ones.

Bulbs are further divided into two more categories based on their climatic requirements. Spring bulbs are winter hardy and actually need the cold of winter to grow (gardeners in warm climates can refrigerate bulbs to mimic winter). They are planted in autumn, grow and flower in spring (except for colchicum, which blooms in autumn), die back, and lie dormant until the following spring. Summer bulbs are tender and cannot withstand freezing temperatures. They are planted in spring, bloom in summer, are dug from the ground in autumn, and are stored indoors over the winter until the cycle starts again. In frost-free climates, they are left in the ground all year. Some go dormant, others don't.

When choosing bulbs, plan for a succession of bloom all year. Start with those that burst into color even when snow is on the ground. These bloom long before trees, shrubs, and perennials add color to the garden and are a wonderful way to put an end to the winter doldrums. Naturalize these bulbs in the lawn, place them in front of foundation plantings or where they will be seen and enjoyed, or grow them in otherwise bare flower beds and borders. Later-blooming spring bulbs can be planted into beds and borders, into rock gardens, combined with perennials, or later replaced with annuals. Summer bulbs can be used on their own or mixed with other plants. Finish off the season with bulbs, like dahlias, that bloom until the first autumn frost. Some bulbs have a nice fragrance, so plant them near windows or outdoor living areas. You'll also want to consider plant height, flower color, and hardiness (detailed in the plant listing that follows) when choosing bulbs.

Bulbs have the most visual appeal when planted in clumps consisting of at least three plants; the smaller the bulb, the more plants the clump should have. Formal gardens planted with stately bulbs such as tulips are best when planted in mass in large geometric beds of the same color. Informal gardens look best when the bulbs are planted in drifts or naturalized. When naturalizing bulbs, make sure they are in a spot where they won't need to be disturbed until the foliage dies down. To naturalize, toss the bulbs on the ground and plant them where they land, making adjustments for those that land too close together. This way the planting will look naturalistic and less contrived.

63

PLANTING AND GROWING BULBS

Whether you buy bulbs from mail-order catalogs or retail outlets, start with the best you can afford. Undersize bulbs will only turn out to be a disappointment. Until you plant them, keep them dark, dry, and cool.

Most bulbs are planted directly into the ground, but some

When planted close together, hyacinth bulbs will grow into a lovely potted arrangement.

summer bulbs (tuberous begonias, cannas, and dahlias) should be started indoors four to six weeks before planting time. The planting times, depth, and distances are outlined in the plant listing that follows. Soil should be deeply prepared (see the section on soil preparation in part

one), rich in organic matter, and have bonemeal or superphosphate added to promote good root growth.

The plant listing also outlines light requirements. Because many spring bulbs bloom before leaves are on the trees, planting them under trees will still provide them with full sun. After planting, water them deeply; this should supply enough moisture until growth starts. Once this occurs, provide enough water to keep the soil evenly moist if it does not rain. Mulching will retain moisture and eliminate weeds.

Small bulbs require little other care, and their flowers can be left to go to seed and drop, increasing the size of the planting. The flowers of larger plants should be removed as soon as they fade to direct the plants' energy underground.

When the foliage of spring bulbs starts to yellow, apply a balanced fertilizer. Do not remove the foliage until it has completely browned. If it is unsightly, push it to the ground and hide it under nearby plants. Summer bulbs should be fertilized regularly during their growth and flowering period. Some summer bulbs (gladiolus and tall dahlias) will need staking and tying.

Many spring bulbs seldom need dividing. When a clump becomes too large and flowering decreases, however, dig up the clump, divide it, and replant it. The best time to do this is after the foliage has browned in spring, because you can tell where the bulbs are at that time. To divide summer bulbs, cut them apart with a sharp knife before replanting in spring.

Tender bulbs must be dug from the ground in autumn. Tuberous begonias should be dug before the first frost; others can wait until frost has blackened the tops. Store them over winter in a cool (but not freezing), dark, dry area. Dry peat moss is a good storage material. Check the bulbs regularly to make sure they are not growing or drying out. Spring bulbs left in the ground all winter will benefit from a winter mulch, which will keep the bulbs from being heaved from the ground.

Hardy bulbs can be forced over winter to bring early color into the house. Once forced, a bulb cannot be forced again, but it can be added to the garden. Tender bulbs also can be forced for winter bloom.

Most bulbs are relatively free of insect and disease problems, but keep an eye on them to be sure.

A GARDENER'S LIST OF BULBS

TUBEROUS BEGONIAS

Following is a list of the most common bulbs, including a description of the plant and flowers, planting distance and depth, blooming period, and hardiness zone (see the map on page 189). If a bulb is not hardy in your area, treat it as a summer bulb and wait until after all danger of frost has passed to plant it. If it is hardy, plant it in autumn. If you're in a warmer area than the highest zone, the bulb may need chilling before planting for it to grow and flower properly, or it may not tolerate excess heat.

AGAPANTHUS SPECIES

(Lily-of-the-Nile)

Rhizome. Globular white or blue flowers bloom all summer on 1- to 3-foot plants with strap-shaped leaves. Plant 1 to 2 inches deep, $1^1/_2$ feet apart. Zones 8–9.

ALLIUM GIGANTEUM

(Giant onion)

Bulb. Globular purple flowers bloom in late spring on leafless stems 3 to 5 feet above basal foliage. Plant 10 inches deep, 12 inches apart. Zones 5–8.

ANEMONE BLANDA

(Grecian windflower)

Tuber. Small, daisylike flowers of pink, blue, or white appear 2 to 6 inches above ground in early spring. Plant 2 inches deep, 4 to 6 inches apart. Zones 6–8.

ANEMONE CORONARIA

(Poppy anemone)

Tuber. Brightly colored, daisylike flowers bloom in summer on 12- to 18-inch plants. Plant 3 inches deep, 6 inches apart. Zones 8–10.

BEGONIA X TUBERHYBRIDA

(Tuberous begonia)

Tuber. Papery, brightly colored flowers appear all summer on 8- to 12-inch plants. Likes shade and moist soil. Can be started from seed. Plant 2 inches deep, 8 inches apart. Zones 9–10.

CALADIUM X HORTULANUM

(Caladium)

Tuber. Grown for its brightly colored and patterned foliage, caladium has elephant-ear leaves and grows 8 to 36 inches tall. Likes shade and moist soil. Plant 1 inch deep, 12 inches apart. Zones 9–10.

CANNA SPECIES

(Canna)

Rhizome. Spikes of bright red, yellow, and orange flowers bloom in summer on $1^1/_2$- to 4-foot plants. Plant 1 inch deep, 9 to 24 inches apart. Zones 8–9.

CHIONODOXA LUCILIAE

(Glory-of-the-snow)

Bulb. Small, star-shaped flowers of blue, pink, or white bloom in early spring on 4- to 5-inch plants. Plant 4 inches deep, 3 inches apart. Zones 4–8.

CALADIUMS

65

COLCHICUM AUTUMNALE

(Autumn crocus)

Corm. Violet, pink, or white flowers appear in autumn on 4- to 12-inch plants. Plant 3 to 4 inches deep, 4 inches apart. Zones 5–9.

CROCUS SPECIES

(Crocus)

Corm. Purple, white, or yellow flowers greet early spring atop 3- to 6-inch plants. Plant 3 to 4 inches deep, 3 inches apart. Zones 4–7.

DAHLIA HYBRIDS

(Dahlia)

Tuberous root. Single or double flowers in all colors bloom all summer until frost on plants that range from 12 inches to 5 feet. Can be started from seed. Plant 4 inches deep, 6 to 24 inches apart. Zones 9–10.

ENDYMION HISPANICUS

(Wood hyacinth)

Bulb. Loose spikes of bell-shaped pink or blue flowers bloom in late spring on 12- to 18-inch plants. Plant 3 inches deep, 6 inches apart. Zones 3–9.

ERANTHIS HYEMALIS

(Winter aconite)

Tuberous root. Waxy yellow flowers bloom 2 to 4 inches tall over deep green leaves in very early spring. Plant 2 inches deep, 3 to 4 inches apart. Zones 4–9.

FREESIA X HYBRIDA

(Freesia)

Corm. Funnel-shaped, fragrant flowers in mixed colors bloom in summer on 12- to 18-inch plants. Plant 2 inches deep, 2 inches apart. Zone 9.

FRITILLARIA IMPERIALIS

(Crown imperial)

Bulb. Stately, drooping, red, orange, or yellow flowers bloom on 3- to 4-foot stems in late spring. Plant 5 inches deep, 18 inches apart. Zones 5–9.

FRITILLARIA MELEAGRIS

(Guinea-hen tulip)

Bulb. Checkered brown to purple drooping flowers bloom on 6- to 12-inch plants in midspring. Plant 4 inches deep, 5 inches apart. Zones 3–9.

GALANTHUS SPECIES

(Snowdrop)

Bulb. Drooping white flowers greet very early spring on 4- to 6-inch plants. Plant 4 inches deep, 2 to 3 inches apart. Zones 2–9.

GLADIOLUS X HORTULANUS

(Gladiolus)

Corm. Flowers in mixed colors bloom during summer on 1- to 3-foot plants. May need staking.

Plant 4 inches deep, 6 inches apart. Zones 8–10.

HYACINTHUS ORIENTALIS

(Hyacinth)

Bulb. Fragrant, dense spikes of flowers in mixed colors bloom on 6- to 8-inch plants in midspring. Plant 6 inches deep, 6 inches apart. Zones 4–9.

IRIS X GERMANICA

(Iris, bearded)

See page 59 in perennials section.

DAHLIAS

IRIS RETICULATA

(Iris)

Bulb. Perky purple flowers bloom in early spring on 4-inch plants. Plant 4 inches deep, 2 to 3 inches apart. Zones 5–10.

LEUCOJUM AESTIVUM

(Summer snowflake)

Bulb. Drooping white flowers appear in mid- to late spring on

8- to 18-inch plants. Plant 4 inches deep, 4 inches apart. Zones 3–8.

LILIUM SPECIES AND HYBRIDS

(Lily)

Bulb. Showy flowers in mixed colors bloom from spring to late summer, depending on the plant. Some have a heavy fragrance. Plants range from 3 to 7 feet tall. Plant 8 inches deep, 6 to 8 inches apart. Zones 3–9.

MUSCARI SPECIES

(Grape hyacinth)

Bulb. Dense upright clusters of blue to purple (rarely white) flowers bloom in midspring on 4-inch plants. Plant 3 inches deep, 4 inches apart. Zones 5–8.

NARCISSUS SPECIES AND HYBRIDS

(Daffodil)

Bulb. Nodding, often fragrant flowers of yellow, white, gold, and sometimes pale pink bloom on leafless 4- to 12-inch stems. All flowers have a central cup or trumpet. Plant 6 inches deep, 6 to 12 inches apart. Zones 3–9.

RANUNCULUS ASIATICUS

(Persian buttercup)

Tuberous root. Lively, papery, swirled flowers in mixed colors bloom all summer on 12- to 18-

CALLA LILIES

inch plants. Plant 2 inches deep, 8 inches apart. Zones 8–11.

SCILLA SIBERICA

(Siberian squill)

Bulb. Early spring brings loose spikes of purple flowers on 4- to 6-inch plants. Plant 2 to 3 inches deep, 3 inches apart. Zones 2–9.

TULIPA SPECIES AND HYBRIDS

(Tulip)

Bulb. From early spring informal flowers to mid- and late spring

formal, stately blooms, tulips come in every color on plants that range from 6 to 36 inches tall. Plant 6 to 8 inches deep, 4 to 6 inches apart. Zones 3–8.

ZANTEDESCHIA SPECIES

(Calla lily)

Rhizome. Exquisite, waxy flowers of white, pink, or yellow appear during summer on 1- to 5-foot plants. Plant 3 inches deep, 1 inch apart. Zones 10–11.

67

ROSES

Roses probably are loved more than any other garden plant—even though they can be the most time-consuming flowering plants for the gardener to grow. This challenge plus the beauty and long blooming period of roses make them popular everywhere.

Roses are divided into several classifications depending on their history and their flowering characteristics. Any class of rose that existed before 1867 is known as an old garden rose. These include the Alba, Bourbon, Centifolia, China, Damask, Gallica, Hybrid Foetida, Hybrid Perpetual, Hybrid Spinosissima, Moss, Noisette, Portland, Species, and Tea roses. Species roses are still popular for their usually single flowers and their resistance to insects, diseases, and adverse weather. Old garden roses are still desired for their nostalgia, as well as for their general hardiness.

The year 1867 saw the advent of the modern rose, the first being the hybrid tea. Its blooms almost

Highly fragrant, the old garden rose 'Frulingsgold' (TOP) bears orange-pointed buds that are creamy yellow. Any number of different roses can be used to create a formal rose garden (ABOVE).

68

always grow one to a long cutting stem and have a classical rose form. Modern roses also include the floribunda, usually low-growing with small, decorative flowers in clusters, and the grandiflora, tall plants with hybrid tea-type flowers that bloom in clusters. Polyantha roses, the forerunners of floribundas, also have small decorative flowers in clusters. Climbers (descendants of ramblers) are plants with long canes that can be trained to fences, posts, or trellises. Miniature roses have become most popular for small-space gardeners, because they are smaller than their larger cousins in every respect. Shrub roses also are grown widely; these large plants are relatively care- and maintenance-free and are used like any other shrub in the landscape.

When selecting roses, it is important to keep a number of factors in mind. If you want roses for cutting, for instance, choose hybrid teas or grandifloras. For landscape appeal, pick floribundas, polyanthas, or shrubs. Roses can be used anywhere in the garden where there is at least six hours of sun (preferably morning sun) each day. They can be grown in their own separate garden, either formally or informally, or mixed with bulbs, annuals, perennials, or shrubs. Early spring-blooming bulbs can be planted between roses to hide their canes before they start to grow.

Plant roses along the wall of the house or along a driveway, or use them as accents by the front door. Larger roses can be grown as hedges or living fences. Choose climbers for growing on fences, especially split-rails, and trellises or against the wall of the house. Miniatures are best where space is limited or in rock gardens, as edgings, or in containers. Also consider plant height, fragrance, and your favorite color when selecting.

Hardiness is another important factor when selecting rose varieties. The most resistant to winter's cold are the old garden and shrub roses, some of which are hardy to Zone 5 without winter protection, followed closely by polyanthas, miniatures, and climbers, which generally survive in Zone 6 without protection. The hardiness of hybrid teas, floribundas, and grandifloras varies; the hardiness of the most popular varieties is outlined in the following rose listing. Some will survive without winter protection; others are so tender that elaborate methods of winter protection are required to keep them alive.

PLANTING AND GROWING ROSES

The first step in growing roses is buying good plants; as with any type of plant, avoid bargains. The plants will be bare root (dormant and without soil around the roots) or planted into some sort of container. Bare-root plants are the type sold by mail-order nurseries; sometimes they are also available at retail outlets. Bare-root roses are planted in early spring and, where climate permits and winter temperatures do not fall below 0°F, in autumn. If you can't plant bare-root roses right away, keep them cool, dark, and moist.

Container roses can be planted any time throughout the growing season. It is best to remove the container even if it is a plantable cardboard box; in summer's heat, however, it is better to plant the box than risk upsetting the roots.

Roses like a rich, fertile, well-drained soil (read about soil in part one). They also prefer a relatively neutral pH in the range of 6.0 to 7.0. Refer to methods of planting in part one. Set hybrid teas and floribundas 24 inches apart; grandifloras, 30

69

Known for its good disease resistance, the climber 'America' is a vigorous, tall grower that's ideal for covering an arbor or training up a fence.

70

inches apart; miniatures, 6 to 12 inches apart; and old garden roses and shrubs 3 to 6 feet apart, depending on their ultimate size. Climbers on a fence should be spaced 8 to 10 feet apart; on a wall, about 3 feet apart. In Zone 8 and warmer, where plants will grow larger, allow a little extra

space between plants. After planting, mound soil or mulch around the base of the canes until new growth is well established, and water frequently if it does not rain.

Roses can be transplanted, if necessary, when the plants are dormant. Use the same timing guidelines as for planting new bare-root roses.

Newly planted roses do not need pruning, except that occasionally a cane will die back and need to be snipped off. Established roses are pruned every year in late winter or early spring when the new growth buds start to swell, except for old garden roses, shrubs, and climbers. They are pruned after the first bloom, and their pruning can be limited to removing dead canes and controlling the shape and size of the plants. In Zones 10 and 11 where plants never naturally go dormant, prune as needed, in early to mid-winter or during the dry season. Dormancy can be induced by withholding water during the cooler winter months if it does not rain at that time. For further information on pruning roses, refer to the section on pruning in part one.

For newly planted roses, wait until after their first bloom before fertilizing; after that, they like regular feeding. They can be fertilized as often as once a month during the growing season but will grow well if fertilized when growth starts in spring after the first bloom and two months before the first autumn frost. Use a balanced fertilizer or special rose food. A supplemental liquid fertilizer can help boost growth and increase flower size.

Roses are also thirsty plants. Water them deeply at least once a week if it does not rain, applying at least 1 inch of water. Water more often during hot weather or if the soil is sandy. A thick mulch will conserve soil moisture. Overhead watering will batter flowers and increase the chance of disease; if you have no other choice, however, then overhead water in the morning.

During the growing season, remove faded flowers as soon as possible to encourage new growth and flowering. If you cut flowers to bring indoors or to dry, you will be doing this already. If you want large flowers, especially on hybrid teas, remove all side flower buds as they form. Also keep the garden weed-free; a thick layer of mulch will help to eliminate weeds. As climbers grow, tie them to their supports as soon as possible to prevent the canes from breaking or becoming tangled.

Roses are prone to attack from a number of insects and diseases, and will need regular spraying in most areas (every 7 to 10 days) to control aphids, Japanese beetles, other insects, black spot, mildew, and rust.

It is best to leave the last roses of summer on the plants to set seed, because this will increase their hardiness. After the first autumn frost, cut the plants back to about 2½ feet tall to prevent wind damage during the winter. Where necessary, apply winter protection after the leaves fall.

Except for miniatures, which root easily, roses are difficult to root from cuttings. Therefore, most roses are commercially grafted. Some amateur gardeners enjoy grafting their own roses.

D rip irrigation is ideal for watering roses: The plants' leaves don't get wet, which will help control some fungal diseases.

71

A GARDENER'S LIST OF ROSES

'BETTY PRIOR'

The following list of rose varieties is organized by classification and includes the most popular roses. Such information as flower color, relative height (plants will naturally grow taller in warm climates), fragrance, hardiness (zones in which plants will not need winter protection; refer to the map on page 189), and whether the rose is an All-America Rose Selections (AARS) winner (an honor designated to certain outstanding varieties after a two-year testing period) also is listed.

Climbers

AMERICA
Orange-pink; medium size; spicy scent; Zones 7–11; AARS.

BLAZE
Medium red; large grower; slight scent; Zones 6–11.

DON JUAN
Dark red; medium size; strong scent; Zones 7–11.

GOLDEN SHOWERS
Medium yellow; medium size; sweet scent; Zones 7–11; AARS.

Floribundas

ANGEL FACE
Mauve, short; very fragrant; Zones 6–11; AARS.

APRICOT NECTAR
Apricot blend; medium height; strong scent; Zones 7–11; AARS.

BETTY PRIOR
Medium pink; tall; medium scent; Zones 5–11.

CHERISH
Orange-pink; short; slight scent; Zones 7–11; AARS.

ESCAPADE
Mauve; short; medium scent; Zones 6–11.

EUROPEANA
Dark red; tall; slight scent; Zones 6–11; AARS.

FIRST EDITION
Orange-pink; medium height; slight scent; Zones 7–11; AARS.

GENE BOERNER
Medium pink; tall; slight scent; Zones 7–11; AARS.

ICEBERG
White; tall; heavy scent; Zones 6–11.

REGENSBERG
Pink blend; short; apple scent; Zones 6–11.

'ICEBERG'

SHOWBIZ

Medium red; short; Zones 6–11; AARS.

SIMPLICITY

Medium pink; tall; slight scent; Zones 6–11.

SUNSPRITE

Dark yellow; short; strong scent; Zones 6–11.

SWEET INSPIRATION

Deep pink; short; Zones 7–11; AARS.

'GOLD MEDAL'

Grandifloras

AQUARIUS

Pink blend; medium height; slight scent; Zones 6–11; AARS.

GOLD MEDAL

Medium yellow; tall; slight scent; Zones 7–11.

LOVE

Red blend; medium height; slight scent; Zones 6–11; AARS.

'QUEEN ELIZABETH'

PINK PARFAIT

Pink blend; medium height; slight scent; Zones 6–11; AARS.

QUEEN ELIZABETH

Medium pink; tall; medium scent; Zones 6–11; AARS.

SHINING HOUR

Dark yellow; medium height; fruity scent; Zones 7–11; AARS.

SOLITUDE

Orange blend; medium height; Zones 7–11; AARS.

Hybrid Teas

BRIGADOON

Pink blend; tall; light scent; Zones 7–11; AARS.

CHICAGO PEACE

Pink blend; medium height; Zones 6–11.

CHRYSLER IMPERIAL

Dark red; tall; heavy scent; Zones 6–11; AARS.

COLOR MAGIC

Pink blend; medium height; slight scent; Zones 8–11; AARS.

DAINTY BESS

Light pink; medium height; Zones 6–11.

DOUBLE DELIGHT

Red blend; medium height; strong scent; also a climbing form; Zones 7–11; AARS.

ELECTRON

Deep pink; medium height; heavy scent; Zones 7–11; AARS.

FIRST PRIZE

Pink blend; medium height; medium scent; also a climbing form; Zones 8–11; AARS.

FOLKLORE

Orange blend; tall; heavy scent; Zones 7–11.

73

FRAGRANT CLOUD

Orange-red; medium height; heavy scent; Zones 6–11.

GARDEN PARTY

White; medium height; medium scent; Zones 6–11; AARS.

GRANADA

Red blend; medium height; spicy scent; Zones 7–11; AARS.

LADY X

Mauve; tall; light scent; Zones 7–11.

MISS ALL-AMERICAN BEAUTY

Deep pink; medium height; heavy scent; Zones 7–11; AARS.

MISTER LINCOLN

Dark red; tall; heavy scent; Zones 6–11; AARS.

MON CHERI

Red blend; short; spicy scent; Zones 6–11; AARS.

OLYMPIAD

Medium red; medium height; Zones 6–11; AARS.

PARADISE

Mauve; medium height; heavy scent; Zones 7–11; AARS.

PASCALI

White; medium height; slight scent; Zones 7–11; AARS.

PEACE

Yellow blend; tall; light scent;

'GARDEN PARTY'

'PEACE'

'RIO SAMBA'

also a climbing form; Zones 7–11; AARS.

PERFECT MOMENT

Red blend; medium height; slight scent; Zones 7–11; AARS.

PRECIOUS PLATINUM

Medium red; medium height; slight scent; Zones 6–11.

RIO SAMBA

Yellow blend; medium height; slight scent; Zones 6–11; AARS.

ROYAL HIGHNESS

Light pink; medium height; heavy scent; Zones 8–11; AARS.

SHEER BLISS

White; short; strong scent; Zones 6–11; AARS.

SHEER ELEGANCE

Orange-pink; medium height; Zones 7–11; AARS.

SWARTHMORE

Pink blend; medium height; slight scent; Zones 7–11.

TIFFANY

Pink blend; medium height; strong scent; Zones 7–11; AARS.

TOUCH OF CLASS

Orange-pink; medium height; Zones 7–11; AARS.

TROPICANA

Orange-red; tall; fruity scent; Zones 6–11; AARS.

Miniatures

BEAUTY SECRET

Medium red; tall; heavy scent; Zones 6–11.

CHILD'S PLAY

Pink blend; tall; Zones 6–11; AARS.

JEANNE LEJOIE

Medium pink; tall (a climber); Zones 7–11.

LAVENDER JEWEL

Mauve; short; slight scent; Zones 6–11.

MAGIC CARROUSEL

Red blend; tall; light scent; Zones 6–11.

PARTY GIRL

Yellow blend; medium height; spicy scent; Zones 6–11.

PRIDE 'N' JOY

Orange blend; tall; light scent; Zones 7–11; AARS.

RISE 'N' SHINE

Medium yellow; medium height; fruity scent; Zones 7–11.

'MAGIC CARROUSEL'

CUPCAKE

Medium pink; medium height; mild scent; Zones 6–11.

HOLY TOLEDO

Apricot blend; tall; slight scent; Zones 8–11.

JEAN KENNEALLY

Apricot blend; tall; slight scent; Zones 7–11.

MARY MARSHALL

Orange blend; medium height; slight scent; Zones 6–11.

NEW BEGINNING

Orange blend; medium height; Zones 6–11; AARS.

OVER THE RAINBOW

Red blend; tall; slight scent; Zones 6–11.

STARINA

Orange-red; tall; Zones 6–11.

WINSOME

Mauve; medium height; Zones 6–11.

75

Old Garden Roses

AUSTRIAN COPPER

(Species)

Red blend; tall; Zones 5–11.

CHARLES DE MILLS

(Gallica)

Mauve; medium height; strong scent; Zones 5–11.

FATHER HUGO'S ROSE

(Species)

Medium yellow; tall; Zones 5–11.

FRULINGSGOLD

(Hybrid Spinosissima)

Medium yellow; tall; strong scent; Zones 5–11.

FRULINGSMORGEN

(Hybrid Spinosissima)

Pink blend; tall; Zones 5–11.

MADAME HARDY

(Damask)

White; medium height; strong scent; Zones 6–11.

ROSA MUNDI

(Gallica)

Pink blend; short; Zones 6–11.

ROSE DE RESCHT

(Damask)

Deep pink; short; strong scent; Zones 5–11.

SOUVENIR DE LA MALMAISON

(Bourbon)

Light pink; short; spicy scent; Zones 5–11.

Polyanthas

CÉCILE BRÜNNER

Light pink; short; sweet scent; Zones 6–11.

'AUSTRIAN COPPER'

CHINA DOLL

Medium pink; short; Zones 6–11.

THE FAIRY LIGHT

Light pink; tall; Zones 6–11.

Shrubs

ALCHYMIST

Apricot blend; tall; very fragrant; Zones 5–11.

ALL THAT JAZZ

Orange blend; medium height; medium scent; Zones 6–11; AARS.

'ALL THAT JAZZ'

BELINDA

Medium pink; medium height; medium scent; Zones 5–11.

CAREFREE WONDER

Pink blend; tall; Zones 5–11; AARS.

DORTMUND

Medium red; tall; medium scent; Zones 5–11.

GOLDEN WINGS

Light yellow; tall; slight scent; Zones 5–11.

GRAHAM THOMAS

Dark yellow; medium height; strong tea scent; Zones 6–11.

LAVENDER DREAM

Mauve; medium height; Zones 6–11.

MEIDOMONAC

(Bonica '87)

Medium pink; medium height; Zones 5–11; AARS.

WILL SCARLET

Medium red; tall; medium scent; will withstand more shade than other roses; Zones 5–11.

77

HERBS

Whether you pronounce it "urb" or "hurb," herbs are valued in the garden for their flavor, scent, or cosmetic and healing properties. Some herbs are used as seasonings in food or drinks, while others can be used as garnishes; nothing will enhance your favorite dishes more than fresh herbs. The flowers of some herbs can be dried for indoor bouquets. They also are common ingredients in soaps, lotions, and other cosmetics; some repel insects. In addition, many people are turning to herbs today to relieve aches, pains, and ailments just as our ancestors did hundreds of years ago.

Depending on the specific plant, an herb can be an annual, biennial, or perennial, and they are grown much the same way as these plants. Annual herbs can be hardy or tender just as flowering annuals are. If they are hardy, they can be planted in early spring as soon as the ground can be worked; if they are tender, they are planted after the last spring frost. Some herbs that are perennial in warm climates can be grown as annuals where winters are cold, and some biennial herbs can be grown as annuals.

Again, depending upon the specific herb, the part of the plant that has herbal uses varies. It can be the flowers or the leaves or the stems or perhaps the roots.

Study the climatic needs of the various herbs before you choose those for your garden.

A traditional knot garden is best designed with herbs that are either low-growing or can be heavily pruned.

78

Some prefer cool temperatures, while others like it hot. Those that are perennial or biennial have a range of hardiness they will grow in. Besides knowing the minimum winter temperature that each will survive, you also have to consider that some must have freezing temperatures in winter. Most herbs like sun, but a few prefer shade, and most like dry soil, although a few like it better moist.

You also should consider whether you want to grow annuals, perennials, or a mixture of both, and what you want to use the herbs for. Think also of the height, flower color, and foliage of each herb, for many add attractiveness to the garden as well as offer their herbal value. Foliage is an especially important consideration with herbs; many have gray or silver foliage, while others have finely cut foliage that contrasts nicely with coarser leaves.

An herb garden can be set off by itself, mixed with other plants (especially vegetables), or placed right outside the back door where you can snip fresh leaves for cooking at any time. One of the traditional designs for an herb garden is the knot garden, where different plants are situated geometrically so it appears

that a knotted rope intertwines through them. Where space is tight, many herbs can be grown in containers. In addition, most herbs are fragrant and are well placed near windows or outdoor living areas.

Herbs are well suited to container gardens and are especially handy when they're placed near the kitchen or back door.

PLANTING AND GROWING HERBS

You can purchase herbs from retail stores, including many specialists, or from mail-order catalogs. If you buy culinary herbs, taste a little bit of the leaf to make sure you like its flavor. With scented herbs, break off a sprig and crush it in your hands, then take a sniff.

If you want to propagate herbs yourself, you can do so by

79

seeds, cuttings, division, or layering, depending on the herb. In the plant listing that follows, the method of propagating each plant is outlined; the full explanation of each technique involved is found in the propagation section in part one. Herbs grown from seeds may benefit from a head start indoors; these are also specified in the plant listing.

The type of soil required by herbs varies greatly with each plant; some like dry, infertile soil, while others like rich, fertile growing conditions. Too much organic matter or fertilizer can ruin the flavor of some culinary herbs; therefore, if an herb likes poor, infertile soil, add no organic matter or fertilizer when preparing the soil. This information also is in the plant listing. Many herbs are killed by wet soil conditions in winter, so make certain that the soil drainage is excellent and that plants are not positioned in low-lying spots.

Planting time depends on the type of plant you are adding to the garden. Hardy annual herbs are planted as soon as the soil can be worked in early to midspring; tender annuals, on the other hand, must wait until all danger of frost has passed to be set into the ground. Biennials can be

added to the garden any time from midspring to about six weeks before the first autumn frost; biennial herbs grown as annuals should be planted in early spring, however. Perennials are planted any time from early to midspring until autumn.

Just as herbs vary in their soil requirements, they also vary in their needs for fertilizer. If an herb prefers infertile soil, never fertilize it. Feed perennial herbs that need fertilizing when growth starts in spring, using a balanced fertilizer. For annual herbs, incorporate fertilizer into the soil when preparing it; no further feeding should be necessary.

Also study the plant listing regarding watering needs. Herbs with average moisture requirements need 1 inch of water per week; adjust the watering accordingly for those that prefer moist or dry soil.

If a plant is growing too tall and lanky, pinch out the central growing tip as needed to keep it bushy. Herbs that are grown for their foliage can have their flowers removed as soon as buds form to keep the leaves more aromatic. Some herbs are weedy plants; you can control them by growing them in containers, by installing metal edgings around beds, or by

removing the flowers before they drop seeds to the ground.

Be sure to keep the herb garden weed-free. Installing a mulch will help prevent weeds; however, moisture-retaining mulches are not recommended for herbs that like dry soil. Some herbs have weak stems and tend to flop over; either stake and tie them, or plant them closer together than normal so they support

Although bitter, both the flowers and leaves of pot marigolds are edible and can be added to soups and salads in small portions.

near or under its hardiness limits, it will need winter protection.

How and when you harvest herbs depends on which part of the plant you are going to use. With culinary herbs, fresh leaves have more flavor than dried leaves and can be snipped any time for fresh use. The leaves usually are also more flavorful before the plants bloom, so snipping off flower buds has an advantage. Harvest leaves for fresh or dried use any time they are large enough; cut them on a dry, sunny morning after any dew has evaporated. Always store dried herbs in an airtight container, away from heat.

If you are harvesting flowers, cut them when they are dry and approximately one- to two-thirds open. If you are harvesting seeds, they often change color when ready, which is usually several weeks after the flowers have faded. To capture seeds, leave the flowers on the plant turned upside down into a paper bag, or cut the flowers when the seeds start to form and place them indoors upside down in a paper bag. Stems can be cut off of a large plant any time or harvested at the end of the growing season; roots are dug in autumn after growth has stopped.

themselves. Herbs generally are not bothered by insects and diseases, but keep an eye on them to control any problem as it starts.

When frost has killed the tops of herbs in autumn, cut them to the ground to keep the beds more attractive and to remove breeding sites for overwintering insects and diseases. Remove annual herbs after frost has killed them. When a biennial or perennial herb is grown

81

A GARDENER'S LIST OF HERBS

The following is a list of the most common herbs. Refer to the Hardiness Zone Map on page 189.

ALLIUM SATIVUM

(Garlic)

Loved by Italian cooks as well as many others, garlic is grown for its bulb, whose sections are known as cloves. This tender annual has white flowers that bloom on 36-inch stems in midsummer. Grow from seeds or cloves planted 3 to 4 inches apart in sun, moist soil, and average temperatures.

ALLIUM SCHOENOPRASUM

(Chives)

The onion flavor of the grassy leaves of chives is an asset in cooking and as a garnish; the purple flowers can also be used. Chives are perennial in Zones 3–11 and grow 8 to 24 inches tall, blooming in midspring. Grow from seeds or division, and plant 6 to 8 inches apart in sun or light shade, average temperatures, and moist, rich soil.

ANETHUM GRAVEOLENS

(Dill)

Leaves and seeds are used in cooking, especially to flavor fish. Flat yellow flowers appear in midsummer on 2- to 3-foot stems. This hardy annual is grown from seeds and spaced 4 to 8 inches apart in sun, average temperatures, and moist soil.

ANGELICA ARCHANGELICA

(Angelica)

A biennial in Zones 4–11, angelica grows 5 feet tall and has white flowers in early summer. It has a celery flavor. Leaves are used as seasonings, especially in drinks; stems and leaves are candied or used in salads; seeds are used for flavoring and oil; roots can be ground and used in baking. Grow from seeds in sun, hot temperatures, and moist soil, and space 3 feet apart.

GARLIC

CHIVES

82

ANTHRISCUS CEREFOLIUM

(Chervil)

Chervil leaves have a slight anise flavor and usually are used with other herbs to flavor foods or in place of parsley. A hardy annual, it grows 2 feet tall and has white

BORAGE

flowers in late spring. Grow from seeds and space 6 to 8 inches apart in light shade to shade, cool temperatures, and moist, rich soil.

ARTEMISIA DRACUNCULUS VAR. SATIVA

(Tarragon)

Tarragon leaves have a delicate licorice flavor and are used in cooking. Tarragon rarely flowers, and when it does, it rarely sets seeds, so it must be grown from cuttings or division. This perennial is hardy in Zones 5–8 and grows 3 feet tall. Plant 1 to 2 feet apart in sun or light shade, average temperatures, and rich soil with average moisture.

BORAGO OFFICINALIS

(Borage)

With young leaves and pretty blue flowers flavored like cucumber, borage is used in salads, as a garnish, or candied. A hardy annual, it grows 2 to 3 feet tall and flowers all summer. Grow from seeds sown outdoors and set plants 1 foot apart in sun or light shade, average temperatures, and dry, poor, infertile soil.

CALENDULA OFFICINALIS

(Pot marigold)

As pretty in the flower garden as it is in the herb garden, pot marigold grows 6 to 24 inches tall and has orange or yellow flowers in midspring to summer. Flowers are used as a garnish, dried, or in potpourri. Start from seeds and space 12 to 15 inches apart in sun or light shade, cool temperatures, and rich, moist soil.

CARUM CARVI

(Caraway)

Caraway seeds are used in baking; the leaves also can be used in salads and the roots cooked like carrots. A biennial in Zones 3–11, it grows 2 to 2½ feet tall and has white flowers all summer. Grow from seeds sown outdoors and space 6 to 9 inches apart in sun, average temperatures, and dry soil.

CORIANDRUM SATIVUM

(Coriander)

Seeds are lemon scented, and fresh leaves, usually called cilantro, have a distinctive flavor. A hardy annual, it grows 2½ feet tall and has white or pink flowers

CORIANDER

in late summer. Grow from seeds started outdoors in sun, average temperatures, and moist soil, and space 10 inches apart.

CUMINUM CYMINUM

(Cumin)

Seeds of cumin are ground and used in chilies and curries. A tender annual, cumin grows 6 inches tall and has white or rose flowers all summer. Start seeds indoors and space plants 6 inches apart in sun, hot temperatures, and average soil.

83

FOENICULUM VULGARE

(Fennel)

Fresh threadlike leaves, seeds, and stems have an anise flavor. Perennial in Zones 9–11, fennel grows 4 to 5 feet tall and has yellow flowers all summer. Grow from seeds in sun, average temperatures, and any soil, and space 1 foot apart.

MELISSA OFFICINALIS

(Lemon balm)

Leaves have a lemon scent and are used in cooking or for drying to be used in sachets. Perennial in Zones 4–11, lemon balm grows 2 feet tall and has white flowers all summer. Space plants grown from seeds indoors, division, or cuttings 1½ feet apart and grow in light shade, average temperatures, and poor soil with any moisture content.

MENTHA SPECIES

(Mint)

There are many types of mint, all grown for drying or for use in food or drinks. Grow from seeds, division, or cuttings, and space 1 to 2 feet apart in sun or light shade, average temperatures, and rich, average to moist soil. Mint is perennial in Zones 3–11.

OCIMUM BASILICUM

(Sweet basil)

Leaves are well-known in Italian cooking. A tender annual, basil grows 1½ to 2 feet tall and has spikes of white or purple flowers all summer. Grow from seeds in sun, average to hot temperatures, and average moisture, and space 1 foot apart.

ORIGANUM MAJORANA

(Sweet marjoram)

The leaves of sweet marjoram are used in a variety of dishes. Perennial in Zones 9–11, sweet marjoram grows 8 to 10 inches tall and has small pink flowers in midsummer. Start seeds indoors or grow from cuttings, and space 6 to 8 inches apart in sun and average temperatures and soil.

ORIGANUM SPECIES

(Oregano)

There are many species of oregano, whose leaves vary in flavor. Some grown from seeds are tasteless, so it is best to grow from cuttings or division. A perennial in Zones 5–11, oregano grows 1½ to 2 feet tall and has pink or purple flowers in midsummer. Space 1 foot apart in sun, average temperatures, and poor soil with average moisture.

SWEET BASIL

FENNEL

PETROSELINUM CRISPUM

(Parsley)

Parsley is a biennial in Zones 3–11 but usually is grown as an annual for its crisp leaves that are used in cooking and as a garnish. If grown as a biennial, it has green flowers in its second year. Grow from seeds and space 6 to 8 inches apart in sun or light shade, average temperatures, and rich soil with average moisture.

84

PIMPINELLA ANISUM

(Anise)

Leaves and stems of anise impart a licorice flavor in cooking and drinks. A hardy annual, anise grows 1½ to 2 feet tall and has white flowers in early summer. Grow from seeds and plant 6 to 9 inches apart in sun, average temperatures, and dry soil.

ROSMARINUS OFFICINALIS

(Rosemary)

The leaves of rosemary are used in cooking, especially in lamb dishes. Perennial in Zones 8–10, rosemary grows 1 to 5 feet tall and has pretty blue flowers in early spring. Grow from seeds started indoors, division, cuttings, or layering, and space 1 to 1½ feet apart in sun or part shade, cool to average temperatures, and average soil.

SALVIA OFFICINALIS

(Sage)

Leaves of sage are used in cooking, especially poultry dishes, and in sachets. Perennial in Zones 3–11, sage grows 1 to 2 feet tall and has violet or pink flowers in early summer. Grow from seeds, division, or cuttings in sun or light shade, average temperatures, and average to moist soil. Space 1 to 1½ feet apart.

SAGE

SATUREJA SPECIES

(Savory)

Winter savory (*S. montana*) is a perennial in Zones 5–11; summer savory (*S. hortensis*) is a hardy annual. Both have a peppery flavor and are used in cooking. Winter savory is a spreading 6- to 12-inch plant with white or pink flowers in late summer. It is propagated from seeds started indoors, division, or layering and spaced 12 to 15 inches apart. Summer savory is grown from seeds started indoors and spaced 4 to 6 inches apart. Both like sun, average temperatures, and poor, moist soil.

TANACETUM VULGARE

(Tansy)

Tansy is a 4-foot perennial hardy in Zones 3–11. It is used in pot-pourri, as an insect repellent, and for dried flowers. Yellow flowers appear in late summer. Propagate from seeds or division and grow in sun, average temperatures, and moist, rich soil, spacing plants 1 to 1½ feet apart.

THYMUS VULGARIS

(Thyme)

A spreading perennial hardy in Zones 5–9, thyme grows 6 to 12 inches tall and has blue flowers all summer. Besides its herbal uses, it often is planted as a ground cover. Its leaves are used in cooking, especially poultry dishes. Grow from seeds, division, cuttings, or layering, spacing plants 10 inches apart in sun, average temperatures, and poor, dry soil.

85

VEGETABLES

When planned ahead—and properly—a vegetable garden can be planted to produce a great deal of food in a small amount of space.

Few forms of gardening are more satisfying than vegetable gardening. Biting into a fresh vine-ripened tomato or serving vegetables you have grown yourself is a rewarding, tasty, and nutritious treat.

With a few exceptions, vegetables are annual plants grown for food; a few are biennials or perennials. Most biennial vegetables are grown as annuals because they are more tasty and tender during their first year. Depending on the vegetable, it may be the leaves, stems, fruits, roots, or flower buds that are eaten. Directions for growing fruits such as melons generally are included with vegetables because their growing needs are closer to vegetables than they are to fruits borne by bushes or trees.

Vegetables are classified as either warm-season or cool-season vegetables. Warm-season vegetables are plants that grow and mature best during warm and hot weather. Cool-season vegetables prefer cool growing and harvesting temperatures and are grown in spring or autumn in most areas, in summer in northern and high-altitude climates, or in winter in milder climates. In the plant listing that follows, each vegetable is specifically categorized.

Planning the vegetable garden is an enjoyable winter pastime. First, pick a site that receives at least six hours of sunlight per day, preferably in the morning. Some leafy vegetables will tolerate light shade, and all vegetables like a little shading if it is very hot. In addition to sunlight, a vegetable garden needs good air circulation, excellent soil drainage, and no nearby trees and shrubs whose roots will compete for food and water.

Make a plan on paper of the vegetables you want to grow. Beginners will find a garden of 15 by 20 feet a good starting point. It is easiest to grow the garden in rows or in raised beds. Plan the garden so that the tallest plants are on the north side so shorter plants are not shaded.

Make a list of the vegetables you'd like to grow, and note whether they are warm- or cool-season vegetables. Select those that match your growing conditions. Also make note of the number of days each plant needs to mature, which is given on seed packets and in the plant listing that follows. Working with this information, you can plan for a succession of crops throughout the growing season. For example, space given to peas in spring can be planted with cucumbers after the peas are harvested. Some crops are quick to mature, and the space given to them can be turned over to another crop; others have a long maturity period and will be the only crop grown in that space. Note in the plant listing how far apart plants and rows should be so you will know how many plants you can fit into your space. Keep good records to help you in planning in future years.

There are several different methods of gardening that will help you best use your gardening space. To make the most of ground space, grow as many plants vertically as possible. For example, stake cucumbers and tomatoes so they will grow upward instead of growing them as ground plants. Succession planting is a method whereby a crop is replaced with more of the same crop or with another crop as soon as the first is harvested. For example, it would be better

A cool-season vegetable, romaine lettuce can also be grown in warm climates if kept shaded.

Green beans that are designated as pole beans may take longer to grow, but they produce more beans over a longer period.

87

to sow carrot seeds every two weeks so you have a continuous supply rather than sowing all of them at one time because they will all mature at once. In interplanting gardening, you plant two crops together. For example, root crops can be grown under or between corn or tomatoes. Small vegetables can be grown in containers.

Once you have made your plan, you have to decide whether to grow the crop from seeds or transplants. When starting from seed, some vegetables must be sown directly outdoors, while others must get a head start indoors. This is detailed in the plant listing. If you don't want to start your own seeds indoors, you can buy transplants at the proper planting time. When selecting varieties, look for hybrids, which have more vigor, increased yield, and generally more resistance to diseases.

It is wise to rotate broccoli with other crops every year and to look for disease-resistant varieties.

PLANTING AND GROWING VEGETABLES

Vegetable gardening must start with good, rich, fertile soil with excellent drainage and a neutral pH. Read about how to attain this in the soil section in part one.

Planting time is determined by the crop and the weather. Tender plants cannot go into the ground until all danger of frost has passed. Half-hardy annuals can be planted two to four weeks before the last frost. Hardy annuals can be planted in early spring as soon as the soil can be worked. Perennials usually are planted in midspring. To plant an autumn crop, refer to the map that outlines the dates of the first autumn frost on page 188. Then determine the number of days to maturity for the crop, and work backward to determine planting time. What category a particular vegetable fits into is outlined in the plant listing.

If you want to start your own plants from seeds indoors, sow them (with few exceptions) six to eight weeks before the outdoor planting date. Asparagus, celery, and leeks need 10 to 12 weeks. Refer to the propagation section in part one about the method for sowing seeds, both indoors and outdoors.

When planting transplants, plant them at the same level they were grown, except for tomatoes, which should be planted deeper. Water them daily until you see new growth, then begin a regular watering schedule. If a late frost threatens tender plants after they have been planted, temporarily cover them with such materials as plastic film or plastic cups so they won't get damaged.

Vegetables are thirsty plants and need at least 1 inch of water per week. If possible, avoid overhead watering. It is very important that plants never dry out during the formation and maturing of vegetables.

Always add fertilizer to the soil when you prepare it for vegetables. After that, fertilize as the crop starts to mature. If growth is poor or leaves start to turn yellow, add additional fertilizer as needed.

Mulches deter weeds and keep the ground moist. If you are growing cool-season vegetables, mulch early to keep the ground cool. If you are growing warm-season vegetables, wait until the ground has warmed up before applying mulch. Plastic mulch frequently is used in vegetable gardens; just be sure to punch enough holes in the mulch for water and nutrients to pass through. Clear plastic mulch traps more heat than black plastic and should be used for growing warm-season vegetables in northern areas, where growing seasons are short.

Remove weeds as soon as they appear. This can be done by hand or with a hoe.

Vining vegetables will need to be staked or tied or grown on trellises or tepees. Tomatoes usually are grown in tomato cages if they are not staked.

Be on the lookout for insects and diseases and control them as soon as trouble is spotted. Slugs and snails and cutworms often eat new transplants and seedlings; slugs and snails can be controlled with bait, and cutworms kept off by placing a protective collar (such as a halved milk container) around the plants at planting time.

A cool-season vegetable, cabbage needs to be fed at planting time and then again four weeks later. The plants may also require mulching to keep the ground cooler in warmer climates.

To enjoy the flavor at its peak, harvest vegetables as soon as they have matured, but while they are still young and tender. Except for beans (which should be harvested at midday), harvest vegetables in the morning when it is still cool. If you can't use your entire crop, share it with neighbors, friends, and relatives, or freeze or can some of it for future use.

89

A GARDENER'S LIST OF VEGETABLES

OKRA

Listed below are the most popular vegetables for the garden. Under each listing is the plant's classification (annual, biennial, or perennial) and whether it is a warm-season or cool-season vegetable. Planting distances, as well as the days to maturity, are also given.

If a plant is tender, do not plant it until all danger of frost has passed. If it is half-hardy, plant it two to four weeks before the last frost. If it is hardy, plant it as soon as the soil can be worked in spring. If a plant is grown as an autumn crop, determine the date of the first autumn frost in your area, and then see how many days the crop needs to mature. Count backward from the first-frost date to determine the planting date. Also refer to the Average Frost Date Maps on page 188.

ABELMOSCHUS ESCULENTUS
(Okra)

Tender, warm-season annual. Sow seeds outdoors, and thin to 18 inches apart in rows 3 feet apart; 55 to 70 days to maturity; okra does best in a hot climate.

ALLIUM CEPA
(Onion)

Half-hardy, warm-season biennial grown as an annual. Can be direct-seeded, grown from transplants, or grown from sets, which are small bulbs. Set 2 to 5 inches apart in rows 1 foot apart; 75 to 100 days to maturity. Select short-day or long-day varieties depending on your area and what time of year you are growing them.

APIUM GRAVEOLENS
(Celery)

Tender, warm-season annual. Start seeds indoors or buy transplants, and space 6 inches apart in rows 3 feet apart. Celery likes a constantly moist, very rich soil; 90 to 110 days to maturity.

ARMORACIA RUSTICANA
(Horseradish)

Hardy, warm-season perennial that can be grown as an annual. Grown from purchased roots planted 12 inches apart in rows 2 feet apart. Horseradish can become invasive; 120 to 150 days to maturity.

ASPARAGUS OFFICINALIS
(Asparagus)

Hardy, warm-season perennial. Start from seeds sown indoors or outdoors, or purchase roots. Plant 1 to 2 feet apart in rows 20 inches

90

apart. Asparagus takes two years for the first crop to mature; after that, plants bear once a year.

BETA VULGARIS

(Beet)

Half-hardy, cool- to warm-season biennial grown as an annual. Sow seeds outdoors in succession all season, spacing 2 inches apart in rows 15 inches apart; 50 to 70 days to maturity.

BETA VULGARIS CICLA

(Swiss chard)

Half-hardy, warm-season biennial grown as an annual. Unlike its relative the beet, it is grown for

SWISS CHARD

its leaves not its roots. Sow seeds outdoors, and space 8 inches apart in rows 18 inches apart; 55 to 65 days to maturity.

BRASSICA NAPUS

(Rutabaga)

Hardy, cool-season annual best grown as an autumn crop. Sow seeds outdoors, and thin to 6 to 8 inches apart in rows 2 feet apart; 90 to 120 days to maturity.

BRASSICA OLERACEA

(Cabbage and its relatives)

Best if harvested when temperatures are below 80°F, cabbage and its relatives are cool-season vegetables. The chart below outlines the planting distances and the time to maturity. Seeds of cabbage, kale, and kohlrabi can be sown outdoors in early spring; those of broccoli and cauliflower

KOHLRABI

	Days to Maturity	Spacing
Broccoli	70–95	18 inches
Brussels sprouts	90–120	2 feet
Cabbage	70–80	1 to 2 feet
Cauliflower	50–70	2 feet
Collards	70-90	15 inches
Kale	60–70	9 to 12 inches
Kohlrabi	50–60	6 inches

91

are sown outdoors in midspring, and brussels sprouts in late spring; collards are sown in midsummer. Purchased or indoor-started plants also can be set outdoors: cabbage, kale, and kohlrabi in early spring; broccoli and cauliflower in mid-spring; brussels sprouts in early summer; collards in midsummer. Cabbage, broccoli, cauliflower, kale, and kohlrabi also can be set outdoors in summer about three to four months before the first autumn frost.

BRASSICA RAPA

(Turnip)

Hardy, cool-season biennial grown as an annual. Plant to harvest after autumn frost. Space 2 to 3 inches apart in rows 18 inches apart; 70 days to maturity.

CAPSICUM ANNUUM

(Pepper)

Tender, warm-season annual. Sow bell or hot pepper seeds indoors or outdoors, or buy transplants. Space 18 inches apart in rows 2½ feet apart; 60 to 80 days to maturity.

CITRULLUS LANATUS

(Watermelon)

92

Tender, warm-season annual. Sow seeds indoors or outdoors, or buy transplants. Plant 4 feet apart in rows 8 feet apart; 75 to 90 days to maturity.

CUCUMIS MELO

(Melon)

Tender, warm-season annual. Sow seeds indoors or outdoors, or buy transplants. Space 2 to 3 feet apart in rows 6 feet apart; 65 to 90 days to maturity.

CUCUMIS SATIVUS

(Cucumber)

Tender, warm-season annual. Sow seeds indoors or outdoors, or buy transplants. Plant 1 to 2 feet apart in rows 3 feet apart; stake for best results; 50 to 75 days to maturity.

CUCURBITA PEPO

(Summer squash)

Tender, warm-season annual that includes zucchini. Sow seeds indoors or outdoors, or buy transplants. Space 3 to 4 feet apart in rows 3 to 4 feet apart; 50 to 55 days to maturity.

CUCURBITA SPECIES

(Pumpkin)

Tender, warm-season annual. Sow seeds indoors or outdoors, or buy transplants. Space 3 to 4 feet apart in rows 6 to 10 feet apart; 90 to 120 days to maturity.

CUCURBITA SPECIES

(Winter squash)

Tender, warm-season annual that differs from summer squash in that it has a hard shell and stores

CUCUMBERS

PUMPKINS

'SWEET CHERRY' PEPPERS

TOMATO 'TIGERELLA'

well. Sow seeds indoors or outdoors, or buy transplants. Plant 6 to 8 feet apart in rows 6 to 8 feet apart; 75 to 120 days to maturity.

DAUCUS CAROTA VAR. SATIVUS

(Carrot)

Hardy, cool- to warm-season annual. Sow seeds outdoors in succession, thinning to 1 to 2 inches apart in rows 1 to 2 feet apart; 50 to 70 days to maturity.

LACTUCA SATIVA

(Lettuce)

Half-hardy, cool-season annual. Can be grown in warm weather if shaded. Sow seeds indoors or outdoors, or buy transplants, and space 6 to 12 inches apart in rows 18 inches apart; 45 to 75 days to maturity.

LYCOPERSICON LYCOPERSICUM

(Tomato)

Tender, warm-season annual. Determinate types have fruit that matures at the same time; indeterminate types produce until frost. Sow seeds indoors, or buy transplants; space 2 to 3 feet apart in rows 4 feet apart; 60 to 80 days to maturity.

PASTINACA SATIVA

(Parsnip)

Half-hardy, warm-season biennial grown as an annual. Sow seeds

outdoors, and space 2 inches apart in rows 2 feet apart; 120 to 150 days to maturity.

PHASEOLUS LIMENSIS

(Lima bean)

Tender, warm-season annual. Sow seeds outdoors, and space 8 to 10 inches apart in rows 2 to 3 feet apart. Likes high heat; 60 to 80 days to maturity.

PHASEOLUS VULGARIS

(Green bean)

Tender, warm-season annual. Sow seeds outdoors; sow bush beans in succession. Space bush beans 3 to 4 inches apart and pole beans 6 to 10 inches apart; rows for either should be 2 to 3 feet apart. Bush beans mature in 50 to 70 days; pole beans mature in 60 to 90 days.

CARROTS

LIMA BEANS

PISUM SATIVUM

(Pea)

Hardy, cool-season annual. Sow seeds outdoors, and space 1 inch apart in rows 2 to 3 feet apart; 55 to 70 days to maturity.

RAPHANUS SATIVUS

(Radish)

Hardy, cool-season annual. Sow seeds outdoors in succession, thinning to 1 inch apart in rows 1 foot apart; 21 to 35 days to maturity.

SOLANUM MELONGENA

(Eggplant)

Tender, warm-season annual. Sow seeds indoors or outdoors, or buy transplants. Space 2 feet apart in rows 3 feet apart; 60 to 80 days to maturity.

SOLANUM TUBEROSUM

(Potato)

Half-hardy, warm-season annual. Some varieties can be grown from seeds; most are grown from purchased "eyes." Plant 12 inches apart in rows 3 feet apart; 90 to 120 days to maturity.

SPINACIA OLERACEA

(Spinach)

Hardy, cool-season biennial grown as an annual. Sow seeds outdoors, and thin to 3 to 6 inches apart in rows 1 foot apart; 45 to 55 days to maturity.

TETRAGONIA TETRAGONIOIDES

(New Zealand spinach)

Tender, warm-season annual is a good substitute for spinach in warm climates. Sow seeds outdoors, and thin to 18 inches apart in rows 3 feet apart; 60 to 90 days to maturity.

ZEA MAYS

(Corn)

Tender, warm-season annual. Sow seeds outdoors and thin to 1 foot apart in rows 3 feet apart; 60 to 90 days to maturity.

PURPLE CORN

SHRUBS AND TREES

Known for their peeling bark, birch trees have leaves
that turn yellow come autumn.

Although shrubs and trees
have their differences, they
have very much in common,
too. Both are woody plants,
which means that with very few
exceptions their tops do not die
to the ground in winter. In fact,
some large shrubs can be pruned
to grow as trees, and some small
trees can be grown as shrubs. In
general, a tree is a plant with one
central trunk, whereas a shrub
has many stems growing from
ground level, but there are even
exceptions to this rule.

Both shrubs and trees can be
either deciduous or evergreen.
Deciduous plants lose their leaves
in winter; evergreens do not.
Within the evergreen category,
plants can be broad-leaved or
coniferous, with needle or scalelike leaves. Many shrubs and trees
have beautiful flowers that add to
the landscape from early spring
through autumn, depending on
the plant. Many have colorful
autumn foliage, bright berries, or
distinguishing bark, adding interest to the garden even in winter.

95

Shrubs can be planted around the foundation of a home to form a transition and enhance the edifice; they can frame windows and soften corners. Low-growing shrubs can line walkways and driveways, while others can be used as hedges, or "living fences." Hedges, which also can be created from some trees, can mark property lines, separate areas of the garden, screen out unsightly views and noise, or act as windscreens or privacy screens. When branches are thorny or foliage is sharp, they make an even better barrier. Specimen shrubs can add highlights to an expanse of lawn. Some small shrubs can even be grown in containers.

Trees form the main architectural lines of the garden; they add

Vibrant bloomers, rhododendrons prefer part shade to shade and can be propagated from stem cuttings.

height and frame views to or from the house. Flowering trees, depending on the type, add color throughout the seasons. Shade trees cool the house and the garden, as well as provide a location for a swing or a bench.

You should consider several factors when selecting trees and shrubs. Flower color and blooming time are important for flowering types; you can select a variety of plants so color is present throughout the growing season. Many shrubs and trees have fragrant flowers that will enhance outdoor living, and the indoors,

too, when blooms are cut and brought inside. If colorful autumn foliage or berries is attractive to you, look for these factors in shrubs and trees. When creating a hedge, select plants with a uniform growth habit, heavy branching, and dense foliage. Plants that make good hedges are outlined in the following plant listing.

Shrubs you view all year or use for hedges usually are more attractive if they are evergreen. This is somewhat true for trees, although many of the deciduous types have interesting winter silhouettes. Consider the mature size of the plant; you won't want shrubs growing so tall they cover windows, or trees so immense they dwarf a small house or spread onto the roof.

Shrubs and trees have specific needs for light, soil, and water; these are outlined in the following plant listing. Choose those that match your climatic needs. Think about winter hardiness also and pick those that match your conditions; shrubs can be protected somewhat over the winter, but trees are difficult, if not impossible, to protect in winter because of their size. Many shrubs and trees must have cold winters to grow.

96

PLANTING AND GROWING TREES AND SHRUBS

Because shrubs and trees are a permanent addition to the garden, soil preparation is critical. Most deciduous and coniferous plants like a neutral pH, while broad-leaved evergreens prefer a soil pH in the 4.5 to 5.5 range. Additional information can be found in the soil section in part one.

Shrubs and trees are sold bare-root, balled and burlapped (B&B), or in containers, depending on their size and where you buy them. Mail-order nurseries sell small shrubs and trees dormant and bare-root, and retail outlets sell bare-root, containerized, and B&B plants. Refer to the planting section in part one for instructions on how to plant these. Timing is a factor here, too; bare-root shrubs and trees must be planted in early to midspring or in autumn, whereas containerized and B&B plants can be planted any time the ground is not frozen. Most shrubs do not need staking, but most young trees will. Read about this in the planting section in part one.

With fragrant flowers in midspring followed by berries in autumn, viburnum shrubs grow well in shady spots.

When planting hedges, set several stakes along the planting line, and tie string between them to make sure the hedge is planted straight. To create a dense and thick hedge, plant a little closer than normally recommended, or set the plants in a double staggered row.

Most young trees are susceptible to sunscald, which causes their thin bark to crack, especially in winter. To prevent this, wrap tree trunks in burlap or tree tape at planting time, and leave it there until the tree develops a thick bark.

Deciduous shrubs and trees can be transplanted in early spring or midautumn when they are not growing. Evergreens take a little longer to become established after transplanting, so transplant them in early spring or early autumn.

Most shrubs and trees benefit from a yearly feeding with a balanced fertilizer. This can be done in early to midspring when growth starts or in late autumn after growth stops. Trees grown in the lawn will probably receive enough fertilizer when the grass is fed; feed others as needed. Be sure to apply fertilizer to the ground under the entire leaf canopy of the tree; this is how far the roots extend. Special pellets that are applied deep into the

97

ground are also good for trees. If the foliage of evergreen shrubs starts to turn yellow, the soil pH may be too high; check the pH and apply an acidifying fertilizer to correct the problem.

Shrubs and trees vary in their needs for water. Those that like soil with average moisture need 1 inch of water per week during the growing season. In most cases, the trees and shrubs in your garden will be watered sufficiently when you water the lawn. Water deeply and as infrequently as possible to encourage deep roots, which will make the plants less susceptible to damage from wind and drought. If it doesn't rain during autumn, water all evergreens well before winter to help them tolerate winds.

If shrubs have grown too large or have grown out of shape, they may need a yearly pruning. If they do need pruning, prune spring-flowering shrubs after they have bloomed (or you will cut off the flower buds), and summer- and autumn-flowering ones when growth starts in spring. Shrubs that have large flowers will benefit from having the blooms cut off as soon as they fade; it is difficult and not necessary to do this with trees. Prune hedges heavily when the

plants are young to encourage dense growth; after that they can be sheared as necessary to retain their size and shape. Be sure the base of the hedge is a little wider than the top so the entire plant receives sun.

Trees are pruned mostly to shape them when they are young; mature trees may need to be pruned to remove dead or damaged branches, to remove branches growing too close to the house or utility lines, or to remove branches to let more light through to plants and the lawn below. Pruning can be done at any time of year and is easier in winter for deciduous types when there are no leaves on the trees; the main exceptions to this are birch, beech, and maple, which you should prune in late spring or early summer because they bleed too much sap at other times. Follow the pruning instructions in part one for further information.

Mulch added around the base of shrubs and trees is attractive, conserves moisture, keeps down weeds, and protects the shallow roots of many broad-leaved evergreens. Don't put the mulch too close to tree trunks or large shrub stems, or this will invite small animals underneath for the winter.

Keep an eye out for signs of insects and diseases and control them as needed. Applying a horticultural oil in late winter or early spring to leafless, dormant trees and shrubs will help to prevent many problems later on in the season.

When shrubs and trees are grown near their hardiness limits, a mulch of leaves, evergreen boughs, or wood chips will help them through the winter. However, it is harder to protect shrubs and trees from winter's ravages than it is to protect other plants, which makes your selection of trees and shrubs even more critical. Shrubs can be wrapped in burlap, but this is unattractive. Evergreen shrubs and trees benefit from an antidesiccant spray in late autumn, which prevents leaves from losing water during winter. If snow or ice gets on your shrubs, remove it as soon as possible to prevent breakage.

It's fun to propagate your own shrubs and trees if you have the time to let them mature; in some cases, it may be the only way to add a particular variety to your garden. Read the section in part one for propagating techniques; the methods of propagating each shrub and tree are outlined in the following plant listing.

98

A GARDENER'S LIST OF TREES AND SHRUBS

FIR

ACACIA

ABELIA X GRANDIFLORA

(Abelia)

An evergreen shrub in Zone 8 and warmer and deciduous elsewhere, abelia grows 2 to 6 feet tall and has small pink flowers all summer. The glossy foliage turns reddish bronze in autumn. Plant in sun or light shade and moist, acid soil. Propagate from stem cuttings. Zones 5–9.

ABIES SPECIES

(Fir)

Firs are coniferous trees that can grow 100 feet tall. Needles are aromatic and flat. They like sun or part shade and moist, acid soil. Increase by seeds or stem cuttings. Zones 2–8.

ACACIA SPECIES

(Acacia)

These evergreen trees grow to 90 feet tall and have fragrant yellow flowers in early to midspring, followed by long seed pods. Grow in sun and average soil, and propagate from seeds. Zones 8–11.

99

ACER SPECIES

(Maple)

This large genus has trees that range from 15 to 70 feet tall.

HORSE CHESTNUT

Some, especially Japanese maple, have red leaves all summer; all have colorful red or yellow autumn foliage. Plant in sun or part shade and moist soil. Increase from seeds, stem cuttings, or grafting. Zones 2–9.

AESCULUS HIPPOCASTANEAE

(Horse chestnut)

Deciduous trees reaching 40 feet tall or more, horse chestnuts have large clusters of white flowers in late spring. Nuts form in autumn. Horse chestnuts like sun and moist soil and are grown from seeds. Zones 4–8.

ARCTOSTAPHYLOS UVA-URSI

(Bearberry)

An evergreen spreading shrub 1 foot tall that can be used as a ground cover, bearberry has pink or white flowers in midspring and red berries all winter. Glossy

leaves turn bronze in autumn. Grow in sun or light shade and dry soil; plants grow well at the seashore. Propagate from stem cuttings or seeds. Zones 2–8.

AUCUBA JAPONICA

(Japanese aucuba)

An evergreen shrub 6 to 8 feet tall, aucuba has insignificant purple flowers in midspring and bright red berries all winter on female plants. Leaves often are splashed or marked in yellow. Grow in part shade or shade and moist soil, although it will tolerate drought. Increase from stem cuttings, seeds, or grafting. Zones 6–11.

BERBERIS SPECIES

(Barberry)

Depending on the species, this shrub is either deciduous or evergreen, and can grow 2 to 8 feet tall. Showy yellow flowers bloom in midspring followed in autumn by bronze foliage and purple to black berries. Some deciduous types have red leaves all summer. Grow in sun or part shade and moist soil, and propagate from stem cuttings or seeds. Makes a good hedge. Zones 3–9.

BETULA SPECIES

(Birch)

Deciduous trees, birches can reach 40 to 100 feet tall. Catkins

BARBERRY

(flowers) appear in early spring. All have interesting, often peeling, bark and yellow leaves in autumn. Birches like sun and moist soil, and are grown from seeds. Zones 4–9.

BUDDLEIA DAVIDII

(Butterfly bush)

Also called summer lilac, this deciduous shrub grows 6 to 15 feet tall and has fragrant lavender flowers in late summer. Grow in sun and average soil, and propagate from stem cuttings or seeds. Zones 6–9.

BUXUS SPECIES

(Boxwood)

This evergreen shrub grows 2 to 20 feet tall, depending on the species, and has inconspicuous flowers in spring. Excellent for hedges. Grow in sun or part shade and moist soil; increase by stem cuttings or division. Zones 5–9.

CALLUNA VULGARIS

(Heather)

This spreading evergreen shrub grows 1 to 2 feet tall, making it a good ground cover, and has pink, white, or lavender flowers in autumn. The scalelike leaves of some varieties turn red in winter. Grow in sun and moist, acid, poor soil; propagate from stem cuttings. Zones 4–7.

CAMELLIA SPECIES

(Camellia)

An evergreen shrub growing 5 to 15 feet tall, camellia has white, red, or pink flowers that bloom, depending on the species, in early spring or late autumn. Plant in part shade and moist, rich soil. Increase by stem cuttings or grafting. Zones 7–10.

CEDRUS SPECIES

(Cedar)

Evergreen conifers, cedars grow 40 to 60 feet tall and have fragrant wood. Grow in sun and average to dry soil. Propagate from seeds or grafting. Zones 5–9.

CHAMAECYPARIS SPECIES

(False cypress)

Depending on the species, this can be a coniferous shrub growing 1 to 10 feet tall or a coniferous tree growing to 40 to 100 feet tall. Leaves are scalelike. Shrubs make good hedges. Grow in sun, average to moist soil, high humidity, and cool to average temperatures. Propagate from stem cuttings. Zones 3–9.

CORNUS SPECIES

(Dogwood)

Depending on the species, this deciduous plant is either a shrub growing 6 to 20 feet tall or a tree reaching 40 feet tall. On the shrubs, flowers are white or yellow, appearing in early to midspring, and white or pink on the trees, appearing in mid- to late

HEATHER

EUONYMUS

HAWTHORN

spring. Some shrubs have brightly colored stems, and both shrubs and trees have red berries in autumn. Trees have attractive bark. Plant in sun or part shade and average soil. Increase from stem cuttings or grafting, and by layering of shrubs or by seeds for trees. Zones 2–9.

COTONEASTER SPECIES
(Cotoneaster)

Depending on the species, this shrub is either deciduous or evergreen, reaching heights of 1 to 8 feet. Many are spreading plants that make good ground covers. Small pink or white flowers bloom in late spring and are followed in autumn by black or red berries. A good hedging plant. Plant in sun or part shade and dry soil. Propagate by stem cuttings or seeds. Zones 3–9.

CRATAEGUS SPECIES
(Hawthorn)

Hawthorns are deciduous trees growing to 30 feet tall. They have white flowers in late spring and red berries in autumn and winter. Branches are thorny. They like sun and average soil and are grown from seeds. Zones 4–9.

CRYPTOMERIA JAPONICA

(Japanese cedar)

This evergreen has shrubby varieties growing 1 to 15 feet tall and tree varieties reaching 60 feet tall or more. Leaves are needlelike and the red bark peels away in strips. Plant in sun or light shade and moist soil. Increase by stem cuttings or seeds. Zones 5–9.

CUPRESSUS SPECIES

(Cypress)

These conifers grow to 90 feet in height and have scalelike, fragrant leaves. They like sun and average soil and are propagated by seeds or grafting. Zones 6–9.

DEUTZIA GRACILIS

(Deutzia)

A deciduous shrub, deutzia has white or pink flowers in late spring and grows 2 to 6 feet tall. Leaves turn red in autumn. Grow in sun or light shade and average soil. Propagate from seeds, stem cuttings, division, or layering. Zones 4–8.

ELAEAGNUS SPECIES

(Elaeagnus)

This deciduous or evergreen plant is either a shrub 9 to 15 feet tall or a tree (Russian olive, *E. angustifolia*) that reaches 20 feet in height. The showy leaves are silvery on the undersides. Small flowers bloom in spring or autumn. Makes a good hedge. Plant in sun or part shade and average to dry infertile soil; it tolerates drought and wind. Propagate from stem cuttings or seeds. Zones 2–10.

ERICA SPECIES

(Heath)

This spreading evergreen shrub grows 6 inches to 2 feet high, making it a good ground cover, and has flowers of white, pink, red, or lavender in early spring. Grow in sun or part shade and average soil. Increase by stem cuttings. Zones 3–9.

EUCALYPTUS SPECIES

(Gum tree)

Although evergreen, gum trees lose their leaves only to be replaced by others, and the bark often sheds. Gum trees grow to 100 feet tall and have flowers in late spring. They are well known for their aromatic foliage, which can be dried. Grow in sun and dry soil; propagate from seeds. Zones 9–11.

EUONYMUS SPECIES

(Euonymus)

Depending on the species, this shrub may be evergreen or deciduous. Insignificant spring flowers are followed by pinkish-orange seed capsules in autumn. The waxy foliage often is yellow variegated. Sometimes called spindle tree, it makes a good hedge. Plant in sun or shade and average soil. Propagate from stem cuttings, layering, or seeds. Zones 3–10.

FAGUS SPECIES

(Beech)

Large deciduous, spreading trees to 100 feet tall, beeches have green or copper-colored foliage. Flowers are insignificant. In autumn, they have nuts and often have golden foliage. Grow in sun and moist, acid soil; propagate from seeds or grafting. Zones 3–9.

FORSYTHIA SPECIES

(Forsythia)

This deciduous shrub grows 5 to 12 feet tall, and its bright yellow flowers herald the arrival of spring. A good hedging plant. Plant in sun or part shade and average soil. Propagate by stem cuttings or seeds. Zones 5–9.

GARDENIA JASMINOIDES

(Gardenia)

This evergreen shrub grows 2 to 5 feet tall and has glossy foliage and fragrant white flowers in early to midspring. Plant in sun and moist soil; increase by stem cuttings. Zones 8–11.

103

GINKGO BILOBA

(Ginkgo)

Often called maidenhair tree, ginkgo has fan-shaped leaves. It is deciduous, can grow to 80 feet, and has yellow autumn color. Although lanky when young, it is an excellent street tree when mature. Plant only male trees because females have an undesirable odor. Plant in sun or part shade and moist soil. Increase from seeds or stem cuttings. Zones 4–8.

GLEDITSIA TRIACANTHOS

(Honey locust)

These deciduous 30- to 70-foot-tall trees have delicate fernlike leaves that turn yellow in autumn. Fragrant green flowers bloom in late spring. Plant in sun and average to moist soil. Propagate from seeds or stem cuttings. Zones 3–9.

HYDRANGEA SPECIES

(Hydrangea)

A deciduous shrub, hydrangea grows 3 to 8 feet tall. One species has pink or blue flowers, depending on the soil pH; others have white flowers. All bloom in midsummer. Prune to the ground in early spring. Grow in sun or shade and moist soil. Propagate by stem cuttings or seeds. Zones 4–9.

ILEX SPECIES

(Holly)

This large genus has both evergreen and deciduous shrubs that grow 4 to 20 feet tall and trees that reach heights of 50 feet. All have tiny white flowers in spring and colorful red or black berries through autumn and winter. Most—but not all—have sharp, pointed leaves. Grow in sun or part shade and moist soil. Increase by stem cuttings, seeds, or grafting. Zones 3–10.

JUNIPERUS SPECIES

(Juniper)

This large evergreen genus has plants that range from low-growing, spreading shrubs 1 foot tall to upright shrubs 15 feet tall to trees 65 feet tall. Many low-growing types make good ground covers. Foliage is either needlelike or scaly. Many species have interesting bark. Plant in sun and dry soil. Increase by stem cuttings or seeds. Zones 2–10.

KALMIA LATIFOLIA

(Mountain laurel)

An evergreen shrub 6 to 12 feet tall, mountain laurel has pink flowers in late spring to early summer and glossy leaves. Plant in sun or part shade and moist, acidic soil. Increase by stem cuttings or seeds. Zones 5–8.

KOLKWITZIA AMABILIS

(Beautybush)

This deciduous shrub grows to 15 feet and is covered in pink flowers in late spring. It likes sun or part shade and acid to average well-drained soil. Increase by seeds or stem cuttings. Zones 5–8.

LAGERSTROEMIA INDICA

(Crape myrtle)

These deciduous shrubs or trees can grow from 6 to 60 feet tall. Flowers of white, pink, or red bloom in midsummer. Grow in sun and average soil; propagate from stem cuttings. Zones 7–11.

LARIX DECIDUA

(Larch)

This is one of the few deciduous conifers. Trees reach 75 feet in height and have needlelike foliage that turns yellow in autumn. Plant in sun and moist soil; propagate from seeds or stem cuttings. Zones 2–7.

LIGUSTRUM SPECIES

(Privet)

Either evergreen or deciduous, this genus is widely planted in hedges. White flowers appear in late spring if the plants are not pruned until after bloom period. It grows 6 to 15 feet tall and prefers sun or part shade and average soil. Grow from stem cuttings or seeds. Zones 5–8.

104

LIQUIDAMBAR STYRACIFLUA

(Sweet gum)

Flowers of these 80-foot-tall deciduous trees are insignificant, but the hard seedpods are attractive and used to make decorations. Leaves turn yellow or red in autumn. Plant in sun or part shade and moist soil. Propagate from seeds or stem cuttings. Zones 5–9.

JUNIPER

HYDRANGEA

LONICERA SPECIES

(Honeysuckle)

The shrubby honeysuckles can be deciduous or evergreen and grow 3 to 10 feet tall. Flowers are pink or white, fragrant, and bloom in late spring; red berries appear in early autumn. Makes a good hedge, but requires yearly pruning. Grow in sun or part shade and average soil. Propagate by stem cuttings or seeds. Zones 4–10.

MAGNOLIA SPECIES

(Magnolia)

Growing 20 to 80 feet tall, magnolias are mostly deciduous; one species, the southern magnolia, is evergreen. Lower-growing species have fragrant white or pink flowers in early spring; southern magnolia

blooms in summer. Plant in sun or part shade and moist soil. Propagate from seeds, stem cuttings, or by grafting. Zones 4–9.

MAHONIA AQUIFOLIUM

(Oregon grape holly)

An evergreen, this shrub grows 3 to 6 feet tall and has showy yellow flowers in early spring. Leaves are hollylike and turn red-

MOUNTAIN LAUREL

bronze in autumn; clusters of blue to purple berries appear in autumn. A good hedging plant. Grow in part shade to shade and moist soil. Grow from stem cuttings or seeds. Zones 5–9.

MALUS SPECIES
(Crab apple)

Ornamental deciduous trees that grow 25 feet high, crab apple trees have fragrant pink or white flowers that appear in midspring, and red or yellow fruit that forms in early autumn. Plant in sun and moist soil; propagate from seeds or grafting. Zones 2–7.

METASEQUOIA
GLYPTOSTROBOIDES
(Dawn redwood)

A deciduous conifer, dawn redwoods can grow to 80 feet tall or more. Leaves are needlelike and turn red in autumn; bark peels in long, narrow strips. Plant in sun and moist soil; propagate from seeds or stem cuttings. Zones 5–8.

OXYDENDRUM ARBOREUM
(Sorrel tree)

This deciduous 75-foot-tall tree has brilliant red autumn foliage and drooping clusters of white flowers that bloom as the foliage turns to its autumn color. Grow in sun or part shade and moist soil; increase by seeds. Zones 6–9.

MOCK ORANGE

PINE

BLUE SPRUCE

ANDROMEDA

PHILADELPHUS SPECIES
(Mock orange)

Deciduous, this shrub grows 4 to 9 feet tall and has fragrant white flowers in late spring. A good, large hedge plant. Plant in sun or light shade and average soil. Propagate from seeds or stem cuttings. Zones 4–9.

PICEA SPECIES
(Spruce)

Plants range from 2-foot-tall shrubs to 100-foot-tall trees. Leaves are needlelike. Grow in sun and moist soil; propagate from seeds or by grafting. Zones 1–7.

PIERIS SPECIES
(Andromeda)

Evergreen, these shrubs grow 3 to 10 feet tall and have drooping clusters of white flowers in early spring. Grow in sun or part shade and moist, rich, acid soil. Propagate from seeds or stem cuttings. Zones 4–9.

PINUS SPECIES
(Pine)

Coniferous plants range from 2-foot-tall shrubs to 100-foot-tall trees. Needles grow in bundles of two, three, or five. Pines like full sun and average soil; some are excellent seashore plants. Grow from stem cuttings or seeds. Zones 2–11.

106

PLATYCLADUS ORIENTALIS

(Oriental arborvitae)

An evergreen shrub, Oriental arborvitae grows 3 to 12 feet tall. It used to be called *Thuja orientalis*. Makes a good hedge, although stems can be weak. Grow in sun or light shade and moist soil, although it will tolerate drier soil and higher heat than American arborvitae. Propagate by stem cuttings. Zones 6–10.

POPULUS SPECIES

(Poplar)

This genus also includes aspen and cottonwood. Deciduous trees can reach 100 feet in height. Brown catkins appear in spring before the leaves. They like full sun and moist soil, but tolerate drought, urban pollution, and salt spray. Propagate from seeds or stem cuttings. Zones 1–9.

PRUNUS SPECIES

(Cherry, peach, flowering plum)

Ornamental cherry, peach, and plum trees grow 20 to 60 feet tall and have white or pink flowers in midspring. These flowering trees do not set fruit. Plant in sun or part shade and average soil. Increase by grafting or stem cuttings. Zones 2–9.

VALLEY COTTONWOOD

PSEUDOTSUGA MENZIESII

(Douglas fir)

This hardy, fast-growing (for a conifer) conifer can grow to 100 feet tall and prefers sun and moist soil. Propagate from seeds or stem cuttings. Zones 3–7.

PYRACANTHA SPECIES

(Fire thorn)

An evergreen, this 3- to 15-foot-tall plant can be trained into a shrub or hedge or to grow flat against a wall. White, late-spring flowers are followed in autumn by large clusters of orange berries. Branches are thorny. Plant in sun and average soil; increase by stem cuttings or seeds. Zones 6–10.

PYRUS SPECIES

(Pear, flowering)

This ornamental deciduous tree grows 20 to 50 feet tall and has white flowers in midspring. It does not set fruit. These neat trees like sun or light shade and average soil. Propagate from seeds or grafting. Zones 4–10.

QUERCUS SPECIES

(Oak)

These deciduous trees can reach 100 feet in height and can have brightly colored red or yellow autumn foliage. They prefer sun and moist, slightly acid soil and are propagated from acorns or grafting. Zones 2–10.

107

RHODODENDRON SPECIES

(Azalea; rhododendron)

Both of these garden plants belong to the same genus, and both have deciduous and broad-leaved evergreen varieties. Azaleas generally are smaller, growing 3 to 8 feet tall, whereas rhododendrons grow 3 to 20 feet tall. Both have a variety of flower colors, but azaleas have smaller flower clusters. Depending on the variety, they can bloom from early spring to early summer. Both like moist, rich, acidic soil. Azaleas are grown in sun to part shade; rhododendrons prefer part shade to shade. Propagate both from stem cuttings. Azaleas grow in Zones 6–10, rhododendrons in Zones 4–9.

LILAC

SALIX SPECIES

(Willow)

The pussy willow (*S. discolor*) is a well-known shrub; other willows are deciduous trees that can reach 75 feet in height. Brown catkins appear in early spring and foliage turns yellow in autumn. They like sun or part shade and moist soil (they will grow in water at a lake's edge). Propagate from stem cuttings or seeds. Zones 2–9.

SPIRAEA SPECIES

(Spirea)

Deciduous, these shrubs grow 1 to 8 feet tall and have profuse white flowers in late spring. One summer-blooming species has pink flowers. All make good hedges. Grow in sun or part shade and moist soil. Propagate by stem cuttings. Zones 5–10.

SYRINGA SPECIES

(Lilac)

These 6- to 20-foot-tall deciduous shrubs have fragrant white or lavender flowers in mid- to late spring. Prune immediately after flowering. Plant in sun and moist soil, and propagate by stem cuttings. Zones 2–8.

TAXUS SPECIES

(Yew)

This genus of conifers ranges from 1-foot-tall spreading shrubs to 60-foot-tall trees. Plants have needlelike leaves and red berries. Compact varieties make good hedges. Plant in full sun or part shade and moist soil; increase by stem cuttings or seeds. Zones 3–8.

108

ELM

THUJA OCCIDENTALIS

(American arborvitae)

An evergreen shrub or small tree, American arborvitae can grow 1 to 50 feet tall, depending on the variety. Grow in the same way as *Platycladus orientalis*. Zones 2–8.

TILIA CORDATA

(Small-leaved European linden)

Heart-shaped leaves grow on deciduous trees that can reach to 80 feet in height. Yellow flowers bloom in early summer. Grow in sun and moist soil; increase by seeds. Zones 2–8.

TSUGA CANADENSIS

(Hemlock)

These conifers range from 6- to 12-foot-tall shrubs to 70-foot-tall trees. They have needlelike leaves. Where conditions are right, they make good hedges. Grow in full sun to light shade and moist soil. They also prefer high humidity and cool climate and do not like high winds. Increase from stem cuttings. Zones 3–8.

ULMUS SPECIES

(Elm)

Vase-shaped deciduous trees have autumn foliage of yellow or red. Many are susceptible to Dutch elm disease; select resistant varieties. They like sun and moist soil and are grown from seeds or stem cuttings. Zones 2–9.

VIBURNUM SPECIES

(Viburnum)

These 3- to 20-foot-tall shrubs have both deciduous and evergreen species. Fragrant white to pink flowers bloom in midspring followed in autumn by red or black berries. Plant in part shade to shade and moist soil. Increase by stem cuttings. Zones 2–10.

WEIGELA FLORIDA

(Weigela)

Pink flowers appear in early summer on this 6- to 10-foot-tall deciduous shrub. Plant in sun or part shade and average soil. Propagate by stem cuttings. Zones 5–8.

109

VINES AND GROUND COVERS

Although not all ground covers are vines, many vines can be used as ground covers. For that reason, the two are discussed together here.

A vine is a plant with long stems that grow vertically or along the ground. It can be trained to climb up tree trunks, trellises, arbors, walls, fences, poles, chimneys, or other supports. Some vines are annuals; others are perennial and woody in nature and can be deciduous or evergreen.

Vines that grow vertically attach themselves to their supports in one of several ways. Some have tendrils, which are modified leaves that reach out and wrap around any nearby narrow support. Others have twining stems that wrap themselves around their supports. Still others have small rootlike growths—called holdfasts—along the stems that cling to their supports. A few vines need help in becoming attached to their supports and will need to be tied with string or

Covered with vibrant orange flowers in late summer and autumn, trumpet vine (ABOVE) attaches itself by tendrils.

If trained to grow upright, ivy (LEFT) can climb to heights of 30 feet.

twist-ties. The way a vine attaches itself to its support is outlined in the plant listing that follows.

When grown vertically, vines can provide color, accent, privacy, shade, and a barrier against wind and noise. They can be used as the backdrop for a flower border, grown up a lamppost, or trained along a stockade, split-rail, or picket fence. They can grow up a chimney or the side of the house; keep in mind, however, if allowed to do this some types can loosen mortar and siding or cause wood to rot. They can hide eyesores, such as the trash cans, or act as a divider between two different sections of the garden. On an arbor, they can cover the entrance to the garden or provide a cool place to relax. Vines also can spill down from hanging baskets.

Ground covers may be vines, but they can also be any low-growing, spreading plant. Some annuals can be used as temporary ground covers, but permanent ground covers, in addition to vines, are perennials or small shrubs. Ground covers often replace lawns; ground covers require less care, and some tolerate light and soil conditions unsuitable for lawn grasses. One drawback, however, is that you

cannot walk on ground cover the way you can a lawn. Ground covers eliminate bare spots of soil, add beauty, and unify different sections of the garden. They are useful on slopes that cannot be mowed, and prevent soil erosion as well.

When you grow vines as ground covers, keep your eye on them if you do not want them climbing onto such things as a nearby fence or tree trunk. They undoubtedly will climb anything in their path.

A very invasive plant, bittersweet can be grown vertically or used as a ground cover on hillsides.

111

In selecting a vine or ground cover, choose one whose mature size suits the area you want to cover. If you choose a blooming plant, pick one whose flower color and blooming period will fit into the rest of the landscape plan. If the flowers are fragrant, this is an added plus in outdoor living areas. If the area is in full view all year, an evergreen vine or ground cover probably is the better choice. Many vines and ground covers do not bloom, but you can plant bulbs or annuals among them to add spots of color.

A vigorous grower, Boston ivy turns bright red in autumn.

Match your plant selection to your climate and growing conditions. Preferences for light and moisture are outlined in the plant listing. Also check the plants' hardiness; although you can protect ground covers for winter to some extent, vines grown vertically are difficult to protect, so pick one that will withstand your winters.

PLANTING AND GROWING VINES AND GROUND COVERS

Vines and ground covers, except for annual types, are permanent plants in the garden, and, therefore, soil preparation is essential. Refer to the section on preparing soil in part one.

Like shrubs and trees, vines and ground covers are purchased bare-root, balled and burlapped, or in containers, and are handled in the same way and with the same timing. Some perennial ground covers are sold in flats and treated the same way as annuals with regard to planting. Planting instructions can be found in the section on annuals. If your vines or ground covers need to be transplanted, do this in spring as growth starts or in autumn after growth has stopped.

It is difficult to state exactly how far apart to plant ground covers. If the plant is a perennial or shrub, plant it a distance apart equal to its ultimate width. If it is a vine, space plants about 6 to 12 inches apart; place the plants a little closer if you desire a faster-covering effect.

Vines and ground covers should be watered to receive 1 inch of water per week if they have average water requirements. Adjust the watering for others as needed. Let your good sense be your guide with fertilizing. If a vine or ground cover is growing rampantly, don't fertilize it. If you want to speed up growth or if leaves appear to be yellowing, feed in the spring when growth starts or in late autumn.

Vines should be pruned at least once a year in early to mid-spring to remove dead branches and control their size and growth. Prune at other times throughout the growing season as needed. When vines are grown as ground covers, it may be necessary to control the direction of the branches. You can peg them to the ground or cover them with a little bit of soil until they take hold. When they are grown upright, you may also need to direct their growth so their coverage is uniform. If they need tying, do so with a string or twist-tie, attaching it loosely to avoid damaging the branch.

Thin ground covers annually as needed, and prune back as necessary. Ground covers may eventually become so widespread they outgrow their space.

Low-growing ground covers can be worked into the landscape in unique ways, often uniting and tying together elements in the garden such as these stones used to create a walkway.

Mulch around the roots of vines to keep them cool and retain soil moisture. Mulch new ground covers to attractively fill in the spaces between them as they grow, and remove all weeds as they appear. Once ground covers are established, weeds will have a hard time growing through them, but remove any as soon as they appear. As with any plant, watch out for insects and diseases and control if necessary.

Ground covers may be protected in winter, if necessary, by raking leaves into the beds or with evergreen boughs. Vines can be wrapped, but this is unattractive and not feasible if they are large, so choose vines that do not need winter protection in your area. Spray evergreen vines and ground covers with an anti-desiccant in late autumn to prevent them from drying out over the winter.

At least once a year, preferably when the plants are not in active growth, check trellises, arbors, and other supports to see if they need repair or painting.

It is fun to propagate your own vines and ground covers. The methods of propagation, which are explained in part one, are outlined in the following plant listing.

Cut them back as needed. A metal or brick barrier will help to keep them out of the lawn or other areas where you don't want them to grow. Also make sure your ground covers don't grow into shrubs, trees, or other plants above them, especially if they are the vining type; they could choke the other plants. The flowers of most vines and ground covers fall off cleanly by themselves, but remove the flowers of large flowering plants, like wisteria and clematis, as soon as they fade.

113

A GARDENER'S LIST OF VINES AND GROUND COVERS

CARPET BUGLE

Below are listed the most popular plants used as vines or ground covers. Their growth needs, plant type, size, flower color, blooming time, hardiness, and other interesting facets are outlined. Refer to the sections on annuals, perennials, and shrubs for plants that can be used as ground covers or vines. Also refer to the Hardiness Zone Map on page 189.

AEGOPODIUM PODOGRARIA
(Goutweed)

A spreading perennial hardy in Zones 4–10, goutweed is a ground cover that grows 1 foot tall with white flowers in early summer. It will grow in part shade or shade and any soil, and, as its name suggests, it can be invasive. It is easily divided.

AJUGA REPTANS
(Carpet bugle)

A perennial hardy in Zones 3–10, carpet bugle grows 3 inches tall and has spikes of blue flowers in late spring. It forms mats of rosette-shaped plants that can easily be separated and replanted. Some varieties have interesting reddish to purple or variegated leaves. Plant in sun or part shade and average soil.

ARABIS CAUCASICA
(Rock cress)

A spreading perennial hardy in Zones 4–8, rock cress is a ground cover but can also be planted into rock walls and crevices and in rock gardens. It grows 6 inches tall and has white or pink flowers in mid-spring. Grow in sun or light shade and average soil. It's hard to divide but can be grown from seeds.

BOUGAINVILLEA SPECIES
(Bougainvillea)

An evergreen vine hardy in Zones 10–11, bougainvillea has brilliant blooms in a variety of colors that flower all year. Branches are very thorny. It grows 25 feet tall; it can be used as a ground cover but usually is not. It needs to be tied to its support. Grow in sun and dry to average soil; protect from wind. Propagate from stem cuttings.

CAMPSIS RADICANS
(Trumpet vine)

A deciduous vine hardy in Zones 5–9, trumpet vine grows 40 feet tall and has brilliant orange flowers in late summer and autumn. It attaches itself by tendrils but usually also needs to be tied. Grow in sun or part shade and average soil; it tolerates heat and drought. Propagate by stem cuttings or layering.

CELASTRUS SPECIES

(Bittersweet)

A vigorous deciduous vine with large glossy leaves, bittersweet has insignificant flowers but produces bright orange-red berries in autumn. It grows to a height of 40 feet if grown vertically and 1 to 3 feet when grown as a ground cover. It is best used as a ground cover on large, barren slopes, because it can be very invasive. When grown vertically, it twines around its support. Plant in sun or shade and average soil; it will tolerate drought. Propagate by stem cuttings. Zones 5–6.

CERASTIUM TOMENTOSUM

(Snow-in-summer)

A perennial ground cover hardy in Zones 2–10, snow-in-summer grows 6 inches tall and is smothered in white flowers in early summer. It prefers sun and dry soil. Grow from seeds or division.

CLEMATIS SPECIES

(Clematis)

A deciduous vine hardy in Zones 4–10, clematis has showy flowers primarily in blue, white, or pink that flower in early summer and sometimes repeat their bloom. It grows 12 feet tall and is not used as a ground cover. It twines around its support but also may need tying. Grow in sun and

moist soil. Propagate from stem cuttings. One species, sweet autumn clematis, has fragrant white flowers in autumn and grows 30 feet tall.

CONVALLARIA MAJALIS

(Lily-of-the-valley)

Spikes of fragrant white flowers appear in midspring on this perennial ground cover hardy in Zones 4–8. It spreads by underground runners and is easy to divide. Plant it in part shade or shade and moist soil. The foliage often turns brown and dies during the summer.

EUONYMUS FORTUNEI RADICANS

(Winter creeper)

This fast-growing evergreen vine grows 1 to 2 feet tall when grown on the ground or 25 feet tall when grown upright. Its flowers are insignificant, but it has pretty orange-pink seed capsules in autumn. Grow in sun or shade and average soil. It attaches itself by holdfasts. Increase by stem cuttings, layering, or division. Zones 4–9.

GAULTHERIA PROCUMBENS

(Wintergreen)

This creeping evergreen shrub grows 3 to 6 inches high. It has small white flowers in late spring that are followed by bright red

CLEMATIS

SNOW-IN-SUMMER

WINTER CREEPER

edible berries in autumn. Grow in part shade and moist soil; propagate by stem cuttings or layering. Zones 3–9.

HEDERA HELIX

(English ivy)

An evergreen vine, English ivy grows 3 inches tall when used as a ground cover and 30 feet tall when grown upright. It does not flower, but its leaves are distinctive and available in a variety of sizes. Some are variegated. It attaches itself by holdfasts. Grow in sun or shade in any soil in Zones 6–10. Increase by layering or stem cuttings.

HYDRANGEA ANOMALA PETIOLARIS

(Hydrangea, climbing)

A vigorous deciduous vine hardy in Zones 4–9, climbing hydrangea grows 75 feet tall and often is seen growing on tree trunks. It is rarely used as a ground cover. The fragrant flowers are white and bloom in early summer. It attaches itself by holdfasts. Plant in sun or shade and average soil. Propagate from stem cuttings or seeds.

116

LIRIOPE SPECIES

(Lilyturf)

A perennial ground cover hardy in Zones 5–11, lilyturf is evergreen in Zones 8 and warmer. It has tufts of grasslike leaves and 12-inch spikes of purple or white flowers in late summer and autumn. Grow in sun or shade and moist soil. Propagate by division.

LONICERA SPECIES

(Honeysuckle)

Deciduous vines hardy in Zones 5–11, honeysuckle grows 8 to 12 feet tall and has yellow and fragrant white flowers in early summer. It twines around its support. It can be used as a ground cover on large slopes. Plant in sun or part shade and average soil. Propagate by stem cuttings or layering.

MESEMBRYANTHEMUM CRYSTALLINUM

(Ice plant)

A succulent perennial hardy in Zones 9–11, ice plant covers the

HONEYSUCKLE

ground with 4-inch-tall rosette-shaped plants. It has daisylike flowers in a variety of colors that bloom in mid- to late spring. It is easy to divide or can be grown from seeds. Plant in sun and dry soil.

PACHYSANDRA TERMINALIS

(Japanese spurge)

An evergreen (in mild areas) perennial hardy in Zones 5–8, Japanese spurge spreads by underground runners and is easy to divide. It grows 12 inches tall and has white flowers in late spring. Plant in part shade or shade and moist soil.

PARTHENOCISSUS TRICUSPIDATA

(Boston ivy)

A vigorous deciduous vine, Boston ivy grows 9 inches tall when grown as a ground cover or 60 feet high when grown upright. It does not flower but has distinctive three-lobed foliage that turns bright red in autumn. It also has blue-black berries in autumn. It attaches itself by holdfasts. Plant in sun or part shade and moist soil. Propagate by stem cuttings or layering. Zones 5–8. A close relative, Virginia creeper (*P. quinquefolia*) is similar but has five-lobed leaves and is hardy in Zones 3–9.

POLYGONUM AUBERTII

(Silver lace vine)

This fast-growing deciduous vine grows 30 feet long and is hardy in Zones 4–7. It twines around its support. The fragrant white flowers bloom in late summer. Plant in sun and dry to average soil. Propagate by stem cuttings or division.

VINCA MINOR

(Periwinkle)

A spreading evergreen perennial ground cover hardy in Zones 5–10, periwinkle should not be confused with the annual of the same common name. It grows 6 inches tall and has blue flowers in midspring. It is easy to divide. Plant in sun or part shade and moist soil.

WISTERIA SPECIES

(Wisteria)

A deciduous vine that grows 15 feet tall, wisteria has panicles of fragrant flowers in late spring. They usually are lavender but can be white or pink. It twines around its support and needs heavy pruning. Wisteria is rarely used as a ground cover but is sometimes trained as a tree. Grow in sun or light shade and moist soil. Propagate by stem cuttings or layering. Zones 4–9.

117

WISTERIA

LAWNS

If you think of trees, shrubs, and other plants as your garden furniture, you can think of the lawn as the carpeting. An expanse of green lawn is attractive, provides a place to rest and play, and unites various parts of the garden. Although ground covers often are used in place of a lawn, a lawn is almost a necessity if you want to walk in an area and not have bare ground.

What type of lawn grasses you grow depends on your climate, how much maintenance you want to give the lawn, and how much wear and tear it will be subjected to. If you have small children who will be playing ball on the lawn, you obviously need a tougher grass than if your lawn is merely a showcase.

Lawn grasses are divided into warm-season and cool-season grasses (see the regional warm-season, cool-season map on page 189). Warm-season grasses will not withstand cold winters but grow well in summer heat. Cool-season grasses tolerate cold weather but

118

often burn out in very hot weather; most of their growth occurs during spring and autumn. Some warm-season grasses, such as zoysia, can grow in the colder areas, but they turn brown in the winter. In the transition zone between the two areas, warm-season grasses can be combined or overseeded with cool-season grasses so the lawn is green all year.

When selecting lawn grass seeds, look for a mixture of different types, such as Kentucky bluegrass mixed with perennial ryegrass. Using mixtures often is better than using one variety, because if climate or pests damage one grass variety, the other type may be unaffected.

In the plant listing that follows, light, moisture, and maintenance requirements are spelled out, as well as the wear tolerance, for each grass. Some grasses spread by underground stolons, while others do not; those that do provide uniform coverage. Use this information in selecting a grass that suits your needs.

119

PLANTING AND GROWING LAWNS

If you are going to start a new lawn or renovate an existing one, the first and very important step is soil preparation (see the soil section in part one). Grasses are permanent plants and will disappoint you in their performance if they don't have rich, fertile soil. Make sure the soil is free of small stones and twigs, and that the pH is in the neutral range (6.0–7.0) for most grasses (any exceptions are noted in the plant listing that follows). Heavy clay soils benefit from an application of gypsum (calcium sulfate), which binds small particles together and makes the soil drain better.

The best time to start or renovate a lawn is in early autumn, when growth conditions are good and there is little competition from weeds. However, lawns can also be started in midspring if necessary.

Depending on your preference and to some extent on the type of grass you are growing, lawns can be started from seeds, plugs (small plants), or sod. Seeds are the least expensive method, but take longer to develop. Sod, naturally, gives instant results. Plugs fall in between.

To start or renovate a lawn from seeds, first prepare the soil, and then sow the seeds by hand or with a spreader at the rate recommended on the label. Do not overseed; this crowds the plants, and they will not grow well. After sowing, press the seeds lightly into the soil with a board, a roller, or the back of a rake. Water every day for about two weeks or until the grass is growing well. When it is about 2½ inches tall, it can be mowed for the first time.

Starting a lawn from plugs or sod starts with soil preparation as well. Plugs, which are about 1 inch across, are simply planted into holes to fit their size. They are usually spaced about 12 inches apart, although they can be spaced closer for a quicker effect. Water well until they start to grow and spread. Sod is laid on top of prepared soil and tamped or rolled into place. Be sure to stagger the pieces so the seams do not line up. Water every day until growth starts and the roots take hold.

Whether working with a new or existing lawn, water as necessary once growth starts in spring. The water needs of each type of grass are described in the plant listing. If a grass has average water requirements, apply 1 inch of water once a week, watering deeply and infrequently for strong roots. Vary the watering of other grasses depending on their moisture needs. Watering by hand is almost impossible. Use a sprinkler or an automatic system, preferably one that works on a soil-moisture sensor rather than a timer. Avoid watering on a windy day, and if possible, water early in the morning.

Fertilizer needs also vary with the type of grass. Lawns require special fertilizer that is high in nitrogen. In the following plant listing, the total amount of nitrogen you should apply per year is given for each type of grass. Because you should never apply more than one pound of nitrogen at one time, take the total needed and divide it over as many applications as are necessary. If one feeding per year is needed, do it in early spring or late autumn. If two feedings are needed, schedule them for midspring and late autumn. When three applications of fertilizer are needed, put them down in midspring, early autumn, and late autumn. If more then three are needed, spread them evenly over spring and autumn, and try to avoid fertilizing in summer's high heat.

A spreader is the easiest way to fertilize. Be sure first to calibrate the spreader, following the manufacturer's directions; that way you won't overfeed. For even application, apply half of the fertilizer in one direction, and the second half at right angles to the first.

Fast-spreading Saint Augustine grass is a good choice for seashore conditions.

Mowing is important to keep lawns attractive and healthy. Be sure the mower's blades are sharp so the grass is cut, not torn. Lawns usually need mowing about once a week but may need more frequent mowing if the grass is actively growing or less frequent mowing as growth slows down. Mow often enough so that you never cut off more than one-third of the leaf blade. The best mowing height for each grass is given in the following plant listing; raise that height slightly in summer's heat to help prevent the soil from drying out. Grass clippings do not need to be collected as long as they are not too long; in fact, grass clippings contain nitrogen and leaving them to decompose on the lawn benefits the grass. After a lawn is mowed, edging it around the sidewalk or planting beds and borders provides an attractive finish.

Thatch is a layer of nondecomposed organic matter that forms on the soil surface at the base of the grass plants. Thatch is not caused by short grass clippings that are left on the lawn after mowing, but by too much fertilizer, incorrect pH, or overtreatment with pesticides. A small amount of thatch is benefi-

cial, because it keeps the soil moist. If it builds up to thicker than 1/2 inch, however, it must be removed to allow water and fertilizer to reach the roots. This is known as thatching, and the best time to do it is in spring, when growth starts, or in early autumn. You can use a special thatching rake, but this is back-breaking work for large lawns, and it's better to buy or rent a power rake.

Lawns not growing well because the soil is compacted should be aerated. In this process, small holes are made in the soil to allow water, air, and nutrients to reach the roots. There are two types of aerators: One drives spikes into the ground to make holes, and the other—and better—actually removes small plugs of soil. The plugs of soil can be removed or left on the ground to dry and then be raked in. Lawns should be aerated in midspring or late summer.

Weeds can be a bane to a lawn, but they are less likely to be a problem if the lawn is properly maintained than if it is neglected. There are two ways to treat weeds. If there are only a few, they can be removed manually or spot-treated with herbicide. If weeds cover the entire lawn, then it is easier and

121

more effective to treat the entire lawn with an herbicide.

There also are two general categories of weeds: grassy and broad-leaved types. Herbicides that kill grassy weeds generally do not kill broad-leaved varieties and vice versa. Grassy weeds that grow from seeds are effectively treated with pre-emergent herbicides, which prevent the seeds from germinating. Some of these can be used when seeding a lawn, and others cannot. Read labels carefully, and ask advice before you purchase weed-killing chemicals for your lawn. Always treat weeds as soon as they appear, before the problem becomes serious.

Lawns have their own set of insect and disease problems that affect no other garden plants. Of utmost importance is identifying the problem so you know how to properly treat it. If you're stumped, your county agricultural extension agent or your local garden center can help.

In autumn, rake leaves from the lawn as soon as possible to prevent the grass from being smothered. If the ground is frozen in winter, avoid walking on the lawn to prevent it from being damaged.

Lawn Insects

Chinch Bugs Circular or irregular large patches appear during the summer, especially when it is very hot, dry, and sunny. The small reddish-brown or black insects can be seen at night or will collect in a bottomless can pressed into the lawn, then filled

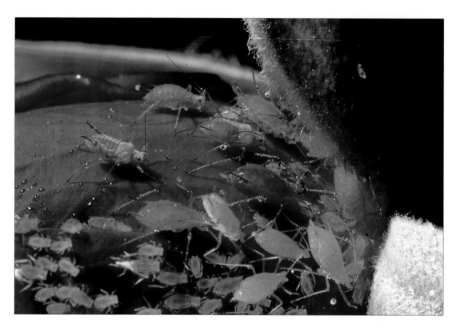

Tiny chinch bugs, which are most visible at night, create patches in the lawn during the summer.

with water. Apply an insecticide as soon as the problem starts, and repeat until it is solved.

Cutworms Starting in spring and continuing through summer, small patches of grass turn brown and die. The leaf blades have ragged edges. The gray, black, or brown worm can be seen at

night on the soil surface. Apply an insecticide at night, and repeat until the problem is eliminated.

Grubs In early spring and late summer, irregular patches of brown grass appear and may be several inches to several feet across. The grass is easily pulled back, and white, curled insects may be visible. Control with milky spore disease or an insecticide applied in early spring or late summer.

Sod Webworms Small patches of dead grass appear in spring and enlarge in summer. Grass blades may be cut off at the soil surface, and white tunnels appear on the soil surface. Moths may be seen at night. It is their larvae that do the damage, and they can be controlled by insecticide treatments repeated until the infestation is gone.

LAWN DISEASES

Copper Spot Spots the size and color of pennies form, enlarge, and grow together, especially in cool, rainy weather, and on underfertilized lawns with acidic soil. Apply fungicides every 7 to 10 days until the problem is corrected, and adjust the pH and fertilizer.

Dollar Spot Brown patches the size of a silver dollar enlarge and grow together, and grass blades have yellow or brown spots with reddish-brown borders. The disease is most active in warm, humid weather, and when lawns are underwatered or underfed. Apply a fungicide twice, 7 to 10 days apart, and adjust watering and fertilizing practices.

Fairy Ring Rings of dark green grass appear in the lawn and may have mushrooms growing in them. There are no chemical controls for this disease; removing and replacing the infested sod is the best way to eliminate the problem. Thatching the yard may help.

Fusarium Blight Large patches of light green grass eventually turn brown and die. The grass in the center of the patch may remain alive. It is particularly troublesome in hot, humid weather and sudden droughts. Apply fungicide three times, 10 to 14 days apart.

Leaf Spot Irregular patches of brown grass spread until the entire lawn is affected. Grass blades have round or oval spots with brown centers and black or purple borders. This disease is most common in climates with moderate temperatures and high humidity and when too much water or fertilizer has been applied. Water in the morning only and apply fungicide four times, 7 to 10 days apart. This disease is also called helminthosporium (after the fungi that cause the problem) or melting out.

Powdery Mildew The lawn is covered with gray or white powder and turns yellow, wilts, and dies. The disease is worse in lawns in the shade and when nights are cool and damp. Apply fungicides every 7 to 10 days, and if possible, remove tree branches so more sunlight strikes the lawn.

Pythium Blight Small patches of brown, wilted grass form, enlarge, and meld together. This disease is most prevalent in warm, humid weather and when the lawn is

Infested sod should be replaced when the dark rings and mushrooms of fairy ring appear.

Sod webworms need to be treated with insecticides.

overfed or overwatered. Apply fungicide every 5 to 10 days until the disease is cured, and adjust watering and fertilizing practices.

Red Thread Thin, red threads appear between grass blades and

Lawns that are overfed or overwatered can fall victim to striped smut disease.

reddish-brown patches of varying sizes appear in the lawn. It is most prevalent in cool, humid weather, when the lawn is under-fertilized or when the pH is too acidic. Apply fungicide four times, 7 to 10 days apart, adjust the pH, and fertilize properly.

Rhizoctonia Blight Large, round patches of grass turn yellow and brown and may have a purple border. Also called brown patch, this disease is most active in hot, humid weather, when the lawn has been overwatered or overfer-tilized. Apply fungicide at least three times, 7 to 10 days apart, remove excess thatch, and adjust watering and fertilizing.

Rust Orange A rusty orange powder covers yellowed grass blades, and the lawn thins out, especially in warm, humid weather and on poorly main-tained lawns. Apply fungicide every 7 to 10 days until symp-toms disappear, and water, fertil-ize, and mow the lawn properly.

Snow Mold Patches of tan or yellow dry grass appear as snow melts. A pink or gray growth may be seen between the grass blades. Apply a fungicide when the disease appears or as a pre-ventive in autumn. Do not fertil-ize in late autumn.

Striped Smut Grass blades turn yellow and are covered with black, sooty powder, eventually causing them to split and die. The disease usually occurs in spring or autumn in lawns that are overfed or overwatered. Apply a fungicide when the dis-ease appears; do not overfertilize or overwater in summer.

Yellow Tuft Tufts of yellow, thick, stunted grass appear throughout the lawn, especially in cool, humid weather. Apply fungicides and don't mow the lawn when it is wet. Also known as downy mildew.

124

A GARDENER'S LIST OF LAWN GRASSES

BENT GRASS

The map on page 189 divides the United States and Canada into six regions based on climate, rainfall, and humidity. The black line that divides the continent separates the areas where warm-season and cool-season grasses can be grown. The lined area indicates the transition zone where either type of grass can be grown, depending on local conditions. Each type of grass in the plant listing has a letter indicating the regions where it can be grown.

AGROSTIS SPECIES

(Bent grass)

Bent grass is a high-maintenance, cool-season, transition-zone grass with fine texture. It has low wear tolerance and usually is used for showcase lawns or golf greens. Creeping bent grass (*A. stolonifera palustris*) spreads rapidly, while colonial bent grass (*A. tenuis*) is upright growing. Grow in full sun or light shade, humid climate, and moist soil. Feed with 1¹/₂ to 2 pounds of nitrogen per 1,000 square feet. Mow to ¹/₄ to ³/₄ inch. You can buy bent grass sod; colonial bent grass is propagated by seeds, and creeping bent grass by seeds or plugs. Region F; A where cool and humid; D if watered regularly; E at high altitudes and in coastal areas.

CYNODON DACTYLON

(Bermuda grass)

Bermuda grass is a medium- to high-maintenance, warm-season grass with dense, medium texture. It turns brown under 50°F. It has high wear tolerance. Grow in full sun in a soil with average moisture and a pH of 5.5 to 7.5. Feed with 3 pounds of nitrogen per 1,000 square feet, and mow to ¹/₂ to 1 inch. Grow from seeds or plugs. Regions B, C, and E.

EREMOCHLOA OPHIUROIDES

(Centipede grass)

This grass is a low-maintenance, spreading, warm-season grass with a medium to coarse texture. It has low wear tolerance. Grow in full sun or light shade and average moisture. Fertilize with ¹/₂ to 1¹/₂ pounds of nitrogen per

BERMUDA GRASS

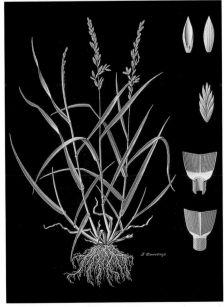

TALL FESCUE

BENT GRASS

FESTUCA DURIUSCULA

(Hard fescue)

Hard fescue is a medium-maintenance, cool-season grass with coarse texture and upright growth habit. It has high wear tolerance and likes dry, acidic soil. It is heat and drought tolerant. Grow in sun or part shade, and feed with $1^{1/4}$ to 3 pounds of nitrogen per 1,000 square feet. Mow to 1 to $2^{1/2}$ inches. Propagate from seeds. Regions A and F; northern parts of B and E; D with regular watering.

FESTUCA RUBRA COMMUTATA

(Chewings fescue)

Chewings fescue is a cool-season grass with medium maintenance requirements, fine texture, and upright growth habit. It has high wear tolerance and likes dry, acidic soil. Grow in sun or part shade; fertilize with $1^{1/4}$ to 3 pounds of nitrogen per 1,000 square feet. Mow 1 to 2 inches high. Propagate from seeds. It is not as heat tolerant as other fescues. Regions A and F; northern parts of B and E; D with regular watering.

FESTUCA RUBRA RUBRA

(Creeping red fescue)

Creeping red fescue is a cool-season grass with medium maintenance requirements, fine tex-

1,000 square feet. Mow 1 to 2 inches high. Grow from seeds or plugs; plugs are preferred because seeds are slow to establish. Region C; warm areas of B and E.

FESTUCA ARUNDINACEA

(Tall fescue)

Tall fescue is a medium-maintenance, cool-season grass with coarse texture and upright growth habit. It has high wear tolerance and withstands wet soil or drought well. It is more heat tolerant than most cool-season grasses. Grow in sun or part shade and feed with $2^{1/2}$ to 6 pounds of nitrogen per 1,000 square feet. Mow to $1^{1/2}$ to $2^{1/4}$ inches. It will tolerate pH from 5.5 to 8.5. Propagate from seeds. Regions A and F; northern parts of B and E; D with regular watering.

ture, and creeping growth habit. It has average wear tolerance and likes dry, acidic soil; it will not tolerate wet soil and does not like high heat. Grow in sun or shade; it is the most shade tolerant fescue. Feed with $1^1/_4$ to 3 pounds of nitrogen per 1,000 square feet. Mow 1 to $2^1/_2$ inches high. Propagate by seeds. Regions A and F; northern parts of B and E; D with regular watering.

LOLIUM MULTIFLORUM

(Annual ryegrass)

Sometimes called Italian ryegrass, annual ryegrass is a cool-season annual grass with medium maintenance needs and average wear tolerance. Grow in sun or light shade and moist soil. Fertilize with 2 to 6 pounds of nitrogen per 1,000 square feet, and mow $1^1/_2$ to 2 inches high. Grow from seeds. This coarse-textured annual grass is neither heat nor cold tolerant but is primarily used for a temporary cover while other grasses are becoming established or for overseeding warm-season grasses in winter to prevent the lawn from becoming brown. Regions A and F; D with regular watering; B, C, and E to overseed.

LOLIUM PERENNE

(Perennial ryegrass)

Perennial ryegrass is a cool-season grass with high wear tolerance, fine texture, and medium maintenance needs. Grow in full sun or light shade and moist soil. Feed with 2 to 6 pounds of nitrogen per 1,000 square feet and mow $1^1/_2$ to 2 inches high. Grow from seeds or sod. Regions A and F; D with regular watering.

POA PRATENSIS

(Kentucky bluegrass)

A cool-season grass, Kentucky bluegrass is a medium- to high-maintenance grass with average wear tolerance and medium texture. It grows in sun or light shade and likes moist soil and a humid climate. Feed $2^1/_2$ to 6 pounds of nitrogen per 1,000 square feet, and mow 1 to 2 inches high. Grow from seed or sod. Regions A and F; D with regular watering.

POA TRIVIALIS

(Rough bluegrass)

Rough bluegrass has poor wear tolerance, but it is the most shade tolerant cool-season grass. It is a fine-textured grass with medium maintenance needs. It prefers moist soil and humid climate. Feed $2^1/_2$ to 6 pounds of nitrogen per 1,000 square feet, and mow $^1/_2$ to 1 inch high. Grow from

seed. Regions A and F; D with regular watering.

STENOTAPHRUM SECUNDATUM

(Saint Augustine grass)

A warm-season grass, Saint Augustine grass has average wear tolerance and low to medium maintenance needs. It is fast spreading and coarse in texture. Grow in sun or shade (it is the most shade tolerant warm-season grass) in average to dry soil; it has fair drought resistance and likes humidity and seashore conditions. Feed with 3 to 6 pounds of nitrogen per 1,000 square feet, and mow $1^1/_2$ to $2^1/_2$ inches high. Propagate from plugs or sod. It discolors in winter when temperatures fall below 55°F. Region C; southern parts of B and E.

ZOYSIA SPECIES

(Zoysia)

Zoysia is a warm-season and transitional-zone spreading grass with high wear tolerance and medium maintenance needs. It grows in sun or part shade, likes dry soil, and is tolerant of heat and drought. Feed with 3 to 6 pounds of nitrogen per 1,000 square feet, and mow $^1/_2$ to 1 inch high. Propagate from plugs or sod. It discolors in winter when temperatures fall below 50°F. Regions B, C, and E; coastal areas A and F.

127

PART 3

SEASONAL TIMETABLES

As the seasons come and go, so do maintenance

tasks in the garden. The following garden maintenance

timetables are presented in seasonal order and then

are broken down month by month and zone by zone.

First, pinpoint your hardiness zone on the map on page

189, and then turn to your zone in the timetables for

invaluable hands-on gardening help and information.

Spring

MARCH

1	2	3	4	5	6	7
8	9	10	11	12	13	14
15	16	17	18	19	20	21
22	23	24	25	26	27	28
29	30	31				

Zone 1

- Start tubers, tuberous roots, and rhizomes indoors
- Check winter mulch; add more if needed
- Press heaved plants back into the soil
- Sow hardy and half-hardy annual, biennial, and perennial herb, vegetable, and flower seeds indoors
- Sow tender annual and vegetable seeds that require 12 weeks or more indoors
- Sow seeds of woody plants indoors
- Prune shade trees
- Avoid walking on frozen lawns

Zone 2

- Start tubers, tuberous roots, and rhizomes indoors
- Check winter mulch; add more if needed
- Press heaved plants back into the soil
- Sow hardy and half-hardy annual, biennial, and perennial herb, vegetable, and flower seeds indoors
- Sow tender annual and vegetable seeds that require 12 weeks or more indoors
- Sow seeds of woody plants indoors
- Prune shade trees
- Prune fruits
- Avoid walking on frozen lawns

Zone 3

- Start tubers, tuberous roots, and rhizomes indoors
- Check winter mulch; add more if needed
- Press heaved plants back into the soil
- Sow hardy and half-hardy

annual, biennial, and perennial herb, vegetable, and flower seeds indoors
- Sow tender annual and vegetable seeds that require 6 to 12 weeks indoors
- Sow seeds of woody plants indoors
- Prune shade trees
- Prune fruits
- Avoid walking on frozen lawns

Zone 4

- Start tubers, tuberous roots, and rhizomes indoors
- Remove winter protection as growth starts
- Fertilize early flowering bulbs
- Press heaved plants back into the soil
- Sow hardy and half-hardy annual, biennial, and perennial herb, vegetable, and flower seeds indoors
- Sow tender annual and vegetable seeds that require 8 to 10 weeks indoors
- Sow seeds of woody plants indoors
- Prune shade trees
- Prune fruits
- Avoid walking on frozen lawns

131

Zone 5

- Start tubers, tuberous roots, and rhizomes indoors
- Remove winter protection as growth starts
- Fertilize early flowering bulbs
- Press heaved plants back into the soil
- Sow tender annual and vegetable seeds that require 4 to 6 weeks indoors
- Sow seeds of woody plants indoors and outdoors
- Sow hardy and half-hardy seeds outdoors
- Plant hardy and half-hardy seedlings
- Prune shade trees
- Avoid walking on frozen lawns

Zone 6

- Start tubers, tuberous roots, and rhizomes indoors
- Remove winter protection as growth starts
- Fertilize early flowering bulbs
- Prepare soil for planting
- Test soil pH; adjust if needed
- Sow biennial and perennial herb and flower seeds indoors
- Sow seeds of woody plants indoors and outdoors

- Sow tender annual and vegetable seeds that require 4 to 6 weeks indoors
- Sow hardy and half-hardy seeds outdoors
- Plant hardy and half-hardy seedlings
- Plant potted or bare-root roses, shrubs, trees, ground covers, vines, and perennial and biennial herbs and flowers, and B&B shrubs, trees, ground covers, and vines
- Transplant roses, shrubs, trees, ground covers, and vines
- Divide and transplant perennial herbs and flowers
- Thin overcrowded ground covers, herbs, and perennial flowers
- Prune shade trees
- Spray dormant trees and shrubs with horticultural oil

Zone 7

- Start tubers, tuberous roots, and rhizomes indoors

- Remove winter protection as growth starts
- Fertilize early flowering bulbs
- Prepare soil for planting
- Test soil pH; adjust if needed
- Sow biennial and perennial herb and flower seeds indoors
- Sow seeds of woody plants indoors and outdoors
- Sow tender annual and vegetable seeds that require 4 to 6 weeks indoors
- Sow hardy and half-hardy seeds outdoors
- Plant hardy and half-hardy seedlings
- Plant potted or bare-root roses, shrubs, trees, ground covers, vines, and perennial and biennial herbs and flowers, and B&B shrubs, trees, ground covers, and vines
- Transplant roses, shrubs, trees, ground covers, and vines
- Prune roses
- Divide and transplant perennial herbs and flowers
- Thin overcrowded herbs, ground covers, and perennial flowers
- Fertilize shrubs, trees, ground covers, vines, perennial herbs, fruits, and flowers as growth starts
- Fertilize roses after pruning

132

- Keep the garden free of weeds

- Prune shade trees and summer- and autumn-flowering shrubs and trees

- Spray dormant shrubs and trees with horticultural oil

- Fertilize the lawn if one yearly feeding is needed, if not done in late autumn

Zone 8

- Start tubers, tuberous roots, and rhizomes indoors

- Fertilize early flowering bulbs

- Plant tender bulbs

- Plant forced bulbs outdoors

- Sow biennial and perennial herb and flower seeds indoors and outdoors

- Sow annual flower, vegetable, and herb seeds outdoors

- Plant potted or bare-root roses, shrubs, trees, ground covers, vines, and perennial and biennial herbs and flowers, and B&B shrubs, trees, ground covers, and vines

- Plant seedlings outdoors

- Protect tender plants from unexpected frosts

- Divide and transplant perennial herbs and summer- and autumn-flowering perennial flowers

- Transplant shrubs, trees, ground covers, and vines

- Thin overcrowded herbs, ground covers, and perennial flowers; thin out seedlings

- Fertilize perennial herbs and flowers as growth starts

- Fertilize roses, shrubs, trees, ground covers, fruits, and vines

- Keep the garden free of weeds

- Spray with insecticides and fungicides if needed

- Water if needed

- Prune ground covers, shade trees, and summer- and autumn-flowering shrubs and trees

- Prune spring-flowering shrubs and trees after they bloom

- Prune and train vines

- Root chrysanthemum cuttings

- Take softwood cuttings of woody plants for rooting

- Layer vines and stems for propagating

- Disbud roses and flowering plants for larger blooms

- Sow grass seed; lay sod; plant plugs

- Thatch and aerate the lawn

- Mow and edge the lawn as needed

- Fertilize the lawn if one yearly feeding is needed, if not done in late autumn

Zone 9

- Fertilize bulbs, shrubs, trees, fruits, and roses

- Plant refrigerated bulbs

- Plant summer-flowering bulbs

- Water as needed

- Spray with insecticides and fungicides if needed

- Sow annual, perennial, and biennial herb, vegetable, and flower seeds outdoors

- Plant potted roses, shrubs, trees, ground covers, vines, and annual, biennial, and perennial herbs and flowers, and B&B shrubs, trees, ground covers, and vines

- Move seedlings outdoors

- Divide and transplant perennial herbs and summer- and autumn-blooming flowers

- Transplant shrubs, trees, ground covers, and vines

- Thin overcrowded herbs, ground covers, and perennial flowers; thin out seedlings

- Prune shade trees, ground covers, and summer- and autumn-flowering shrubs and trees

- Prune spring-flowering shrubs and trees after they bloom

- Prune and train vines

- Shear fine-needled evergreens as needed

133

- Fertilize perennial herbs and flowers as growth starts

- Keep the garden free of weeds

- Apply summer mulch

- Stake tall plants

- Harvest herb leaves and seeds

- Harvest vegetables and fruits when ripe

- Cut flowers for fresh use or drying

- Disbud roses and other flowering plants for larger blooms

- Remove faded flowers

- Sow grass seed; lay sod; plant plugs

- Thatch and aerate the lawn

- Mow and edge the lawn as needed

- Fertilize the lawn for the first time if two or three yearly applications are needed

Zone 10

- Fertilize bulbs, shrubs, trees, fruits, and roses

- Plant refrigerated bulbs

- Plant summer-flowering bulbs

- Water as needed

- Spray with insecticides and fungicides if needed

- Sow annual, perennial, and biennial herb, vegetable, and flower seeds outdoors

- Plant potted roses, shrubs, trees, ground covers, vines, and annual, biennial, and perennial herbs and flowers, and B&B shrubs, trees, ground covers, and vines

- Move seedlings outdoors

- Divide and transplant perennial herbs and summer- and autumn-blooming flowers

- Transplant shrubs, trees, ground covers, and vines

- Thin overcrowded herbs, ground covers, and perennial flowers; thin seedlings

- Prune shade trees, ground covers, and summer- and autumn-flowering shrubs and trees

- Prune spring-flowering shrubs and trees after they bloom

- Prune and train vines

- Shear fine-needled evergreens as needed

- Fertilize perennial herbs and flowers as growth starts

- Keep the garden free of weeds

- Apply summer mulch

- Stake tall plants

- Harvest herb leaves and seeds

- Cut flowers for fresh use or drying

- Harvest vegetables and fruits when ripe

- Disbud roses and other flowering plants for larger blooms

- Remove faded flowers

- Sow grass seed; lay sod; plant plugs

- Thatch and aerate the lawn

- Mow and edge the lawn as needed

- Fertilize the lawn for the first time if two or three yearly applications are needed

Zone 11

- Fertilize bulbs, shrubs, trees, fruits, and roses

- Plant refrigerated bulbs

- Plant summer-flowering bulbs

- Water as needed

- Spray with insecticides and fungicides if needed

- Sow annual, perennial, and biennial herb, vegetable, and flower seeds outdoors

- Plant potted roses, shrubs, trees, ground covers, vines, and annual, biennial, and perennial herbs and flowers, and B&B shrubs, trees, ground covers, and vines

- Move seedlings outdoors

- Divide and transplant perennial herbs and summer- and autumn-blooming flowers

- Transplant shrubs, trees, ground covers, and vines

- Thin overcrowded herbs, ground covers, and perennial flowers; thin seedlings

- Prune shade trees, ground covers, and summer- and autumn-flowering shrubs and trees

- Prune spring-flowering shrubs and trees after they bloom

- Prune and train vines

- Shear fine-needled evergreens as needed

- Fertilize perennial herbs and flowers as growth starts

- Keep the garden free of weeds

- Apply summer mulch

- Stake tall plants

- Harvest herb leaves and seeds

- Harvest vegetables and fruits when ripe

- Cut flowers for fresh use or drying

- Disbud roses and other flowering plants for larger blooms

- Remove faded flowers

- Sow grass seed; lay sod; plant plugs

- Thatch and aerate the lawn

- Mow and edge the lawn as needed

- Fertilize the lawn for the first time if two or three yearly applications are needed

APRIL

1	2	3	4	5	6	7
8	9	10	11	12	13	14
15	16	17	18	19	20	21
22	23	24	25	26	27	28
29	30					

Zone 1

- Remove winter protection as growth starts

- Fertilize early flowering bulbs

- Start rhizomes, tubers, and tuberous roots indoors

- Prepare soil for planting

- Test soil pH; adjust if needed

- Sow perennial and biennial herb and flower seeds indoors

- Sow hardy and half-hardy annual flower and vegetable seeds indoors

- Sow tender annual flower and vegetable seeds that require 6 to 10 weeks indoors

- Plant potted or bare-root roses, shrubs, trees, ground covers, vines, and perennial and biennial herbs and flowers, and B&B shrubs, trees, ground covers, and vines

- Transplant roses, shrubs, trees, ground covers, and vines

- Prune roses and ground covers

- Train and prune vines

- Prune shade trees and summer- and autumn-flowering shrubs and trees

- Fertilize roses after pruning

- Thin overcrowded herbs, perennial flowers, and ground covers

- Fertilize shrubs, trees, ground covers, vines, fruits, and perennial herbs and flowers as growth starts

- Keep the garden free of weeds

- Spray dormant shrubs and trees with horticultural oil

- Sow grass seed; lay sod; plant plugs

- Thatch and aerate the lawn

- Mow and edge the lawn as needed

- Fertilize the lawn if one yearly feeding is needed, if not done in late autumn

Zone 2

- Remove winter protection as growth starts

- Fertilize early flowering bulbs

- Start rhizomes, tubers, and tuberous roots indoors

135

- Prepare soil for planting

- Test soil pH; adjust if needed

- Sow perennial and biennial herb and flower seeds indoors

- Sow hardy and half-hardy annual flower and vegetable seeds indoors

- Sow tender annual flower and vegetable seeds that require 6 to 10 weeks indoors

- Plant potted or bare-root roses, shrubs, trees, ground covers, vines, and perennial and biennial herbs and flowers, and B&B shrubs, trees, ground covers, and vines

- Transplant roses, shrubs, trees, ground covers, vines, and perennial flowers

- Prune roses and ground covers

- Prune shade trees and summer- and autumn-flowering shrubs and trees

- Train and prune vines

- Fertilize roses after pruning

- Thin overcrowded herbs, perennial flowers, and ground covers

- Fertilize shrubs, trees, ground covers, vines, fruits, and perennial herbs and flowers as growth starts

- Keep the garden free of weeds

- Spray dormant shrubs and trees with horticultural oil

- Sow grass seed; lay sod; plant plugs

- Thatch and aerate the lawn

- Mow and edge the lawn as needed

- Fertilize the lawn if one yearly feeding is needed, if not done in late autumn

Zone 3

- Remove winter protection as growth starts

- Fertilize early flowering bulbs

- Start rhizomes, tubers, and tuberous roots indoors

- Prepare soil for planting

- Test soil pH; adjust if needed

- Sow perennial and biennial herb and flower seeds indoors

- Sow tender annual flower and vegetable seeds that require 4 to 6 weeks indoors

- Plant potted or bare-root roses, shrubs, trees, ground covers, vines, and perennial and biennial herbs and flowers, and B&B shrubs, trees, ground covers, and vines

- Thin overcrowded plantings of herbs, perennial flowers, and ground covers

- Fertilize shrubs, trees, ground covers, vines, fruits, and perennial herbs and flowers as growth starts

- Transplant roses, shrubs, trees, ground covers, and vines

- Prune roses and ground covers

- Prune shade trees and summer- and autumn-flowering shrubs and trees

- Train and prune vines

- Fertilize roses after pruning

- Keep the garden free of weeds

- Spray dormant shrubs and trees with horticultural oil

- Sow grass seed; lay sod; plant plugs

- Thatch and aerate the lawn

- Mow and edge the lawn as needed

- Fertilize the lawn if one yearly feeding is needed, if not done in late autumn

Zone 4

- Remove winter protection as growth starts

- Transplant and divide early flowering bulbs

- Prepare soil for planting

- Test soil pH; adjust if needed

- Sow annual, perennial, and biennial seeds indoors

- Sow hardy and half-hardy annual flower and vegetable seeds outdoors

- Plant hardy and half-hardy annual flower and vegetable seedlings outdoors

- Plant potted or bare-root roses, shrubs, trees, ground covers, vines, perennial and biennial herbs and flowers, and B&B shrubs, trees, ground covers, and vines

- Transplant roses, shrubs, trees, ground covers, and vines

- Prune roses and ground covers

- Prune shade trees and summer- and autumn-flowering shrubs and trees

- Train and prune vines

- Fertilize roses after pruning

- Thin overcrowded herbs, perennial flowers, and ground covers

- Fertilize shrubs, trees, ground covers, vines, fruits, and perennial herbs and flowers as growth starts

- Keep the garden free of weeds

- Spray dormant shrubs and trees with horticultural oil

- Sow grass seed; lay sod; plant plugs

- Thatch and aerate the lawn

- Mow and edge the lawn as needed

- Fertilize the lawn if one yearly feeding is needed, if not done in late autumn

Zone 5

- Remove winter protection as growth starts

- Transplant and divide early flowering bulbs

- Prepare soil for planting

- Test soil pH; adjust if needed

- Sow perennial and biennial herb and flower seeds indoors

- Sow hardy and half-hardy annual flower and vegetable seeds outdoors

- Plant hardy and half-hardy seedlings outdoors

- Plant potted or bare-root roses, shrubs, trees, ground covers, vines, and perennial and biennial herbs and flowers, and B&B shrubs, trees, ground covers, and vines

- Transplant roses, shrubs, trees, ground covers, and vines

- Protect tender plants from unexpected frosts if needed

- Prune roses and ground covers

- Prune shade trees and summer- and autumn-flowering shrubs and trees

- Train and prune vines

- Fertilize roses after pruning

- Thin overcrowded herbs, perennial flowers, and ground covers

- Fertilize shrubs, trees, ground covers, vines, fruits, and perennial herbs and flowers as growth starts

- Keep the garden free of weeds

- Spray dormant shrubs and trees with horticultural oil

- Sow grass seed; lay sod; plant plugs

- Thatch and aerate the lawn

- Mow and edge the lawn as needed

- Fertilize the lawn if one yearly feeding is needed, if not done in late autumn

Zone 6

- Remove winter protection as growth starts

- Transplant and divide early flowering bulbs

- Fertilize early flowering bulbs

- Plant forced bulbs outdoors

- Prepare soil for planting

- Test soil pH; adjust if needed

- Sow perennial and biennial herb and flower seeds indoors or outdoors

- Sow hardy and half-hardy annual and vegetable seeds outdoors

- Move hardy and half-hardy seedlings outdoors

- Plant potted or bare-root roses, shrubs, trees, ground covers, vines, and perennial and biennial herbs and flowers, and B&B shrubs, trees, ground covers, and vines

- Transplant roses, shrubs, trees, ground covers, and vines

- Protect tender plants from unexpected frosts if needed

- Prune roses and ground covers

- Prune shade trees and summer- and autumn-flowering shrubs and trees

- Train and prune vines

- Fertilize roses after pruning

- Thin overcrowded herbs, perennial flowers, seedlings, and ground covers

- Fertilize shrubs, trees, ground covers, vines, fruits, and perennial herbs and flowers as growth starts

- Keep the garden free of weeds

- Spray dormant shrubs and trees with horticultural oil

- Sow grass seed; lay sod; plant plugs

- Thatch and aerate the lawn

- Mow and edge the lawn as needed

- Fertilize the lawn if one yearly feeding is needed, if not done in late autumn

Zone 7

- Transplant and divide early flowering bulbs

- Fertilize early flowering bulbs

- Plant forced bulbs outdoors

- Prepare soil for planting

- Test soil pH; adjust if needed

- Sow perennial and biennial herb and flower seeds indoors and outdoors

- Sow hardy and half-hardy seeds outdoors

- Move hardy and half-hardy seedlings outdoors

- Plant potted or bare-root roses, shrubs, trees, ground covers, vines, and perennial and biennial herbs and flowers, and B&B shrubs, trees, ground covers, and vines

- Transplant roses, shrubs, trees, ground covers, and vines

- Protect tender plants from unexpected frosts if needed

- Prune roses and ground covers

- Prune shade trees and summer- and autumn-flowering shrubs and trees

- Prune spring-flowering shrubs and trees after they bloom

- Train and prune vines

- Fertilize roses after pruning

- Divide and transplant perennial herbs, flowers, and ground covers

- Thin overcrowded herbs, perennial flowers, seedlings, and ground covers

- Fertilize shrubs, trees, ground covers, vines, fruits, and perennial herbs and flowers as growth starts

- Stake tall plants

- Keep the garden free of weeds

- Spray with insecticides and fungicides if needed

- Sow grass seed; lay sod; plant plugs

- Thatch and aerate the lawn

- Mow and edge the lawn as needed

- Fertilize the lawn if one yearly feeding is needed, if not done in late autumn

- Fertilize the lawn for the first time if two or three yearly feedings are needed

Zone 8

- Transplant and divide early flowering bulbs

- Fertilize early flowering bulbs

- Plant summer-flowering bulbs

- Sow annual, biennial, and perennial herb and flower seeds outdoors

- Plant potted roses, shrubs, trees, ground covers, vines, herbs, and perennial flowers, and B&B shrubs, trees, ground covers, and vines

- Move seedlings outdoors

- Thin seedlings

- Prune shade trees and summer- and autumn-flowering shrubs and trees

- Shear fine-needled evergreens as needed

- Prune spring-flowering shrubs and trees after they bloom

- Prune ground covers if needed; train and prune vines

- Water as needed

- Spray with insecticides and fungicides if needed

- Keep the garden free of weeds

- Apply summer mulch

- Stake tall plants

- Fertilize roses; fertilize other plants as needed

- Remove faded flowers

- Disbud roses and other flowers for larger blooms

- Move rooted chrysanthemums outdoors

- Lay sod; plant plugs

- Mow and edge the lawn as needed

- Fertilize the lawn for the first time if two or three yearly feedings are needed

Zone 9

- Transplant and divide early flowering bulbs

- Fertilize early flowering bulbs

- Plant summer-flowering bulbs

- Plant potted roses, shrubs, trees, ground covers, vines, herbs, and perennial flowers, and B&B shrubs, trees, ground covers, and vines

- Prune shade trees and summer- and autumn-flowering shrubs and trees

- Prune spring-flowering shrubs and trees after they bloom

- Prune ground covers if needed; train and prune vines

- Keep the garden free of weeds

- Sow annual, biennial, and perennial seeds outdoors

- Move seedlings outdoors

- Thin seedlings

- Harvest herb leaves and seeds

- Harvest vegetables and fruits when ripe

- Cut flowers for fresh use or drying

- Water as needed

- Spray with insecticides and fungicides if needed

- Fertilize roses; fertilize other plants as needed

- Disbud roses and other flowering plants for larger blooms

- Remove faded flowers

- Plant chrysanthemums

- Pinch annuals and perennials as needed

- Lay sod; plant plugs

- Mow and edge the lawn as needed

Zone 10

- Transplant and divide early flowering bulbs

- Fertilize early flowering bulbs

- Plant summer-flowering bulbs

- Plant potted roses, shrubs, trees, ground covers, vines, herbs, and perennial flowers, and B&B shrubs, trees, ground covers, and vines

- Prune shade trees and summer- and autumn-flowering shrubs and trees

- Prune spring-flowering shrubs and trees after they bloom

- Prune ground covers if needed; train and prune vines

- Keep the garden free of weeds

- Sow annual, biennial, and perennial seeds outdoors

- Move seedlings outdoors

139

- Thin seedlings

- Harvest herb leaves and seeds

- Harvest vegetables and fruits when ripe

- Cut flowers for fresh use or drying

- Water as needed

- Spray with insecticides and fungicides if needed

- Fertilize roses; fertilize other plants as needed

- Disbud roses and other flowering plants for larger blooms

- Remove faded flowers

- Plant chrysanthemums

- Pinch annuals and perennials as needed

- Lay sod; plant plugs

- Mow and edge the lawn as needed

Zone 11

- Transplant and divide early flowering bulbs

- Fertilize early flowering bulbs

- Plant summer-flowering bulbs

- Plant potted roses, shrubs, trees, ground covers, vines, herbs, and perennial flowers, and B&B shrubs, trees, ground covers, and vines

- Prune shade trees and summer- and autumn-flowering shrubs and trees

- Prune spring-flowering shrubs and trees after they bloom

- Prune ground covers if needed; train and prune vines

- Keep the garden free of weeds

- Sow annual, biennial, and perennial seeds outdoors

- Move seedlings outdoors

- Harvest herb leaves and seeds

- Harvest vegetables and fruits when ripe

- Cut flowers for fresh use or drying

- Water as needed

- Spray with insecticides and fungicides if needed

- Fertilize roses; fertilize other plants as needed

- Disbud roses and other flowering plants for larger blooms

- Remove faded flowers

- Plant chrysanthemums

- Pinch annuals and perennials as needed

- Lay sod; plant plugs

- Mow and edge the lawn as needed

MAY

1	2	3	4	5	6	7
8	9	10	11	12	13	14
15	16	17	18	19	20	21
22	23	24	25	26	27	28
29	30	31				

Zone 1

- Prepare soil for planting

- Fertilize roses and early flowering bulbs

- Divide and transplant early flowering bulbs

- Sow perennial and biennial herb and flower seeds outdoors

- Sow hardy and half-hardy annual and vegetable seeds outdoors

- Sow tender annual and vegetable seeds that require 4 to 6 weeks indoors

- Plant potted or bare-root roses, shrubs, trees, ground covers, vines, and perennial and biennial herbs and flowers, and B&B shrubs, trees, ground covers, and vines

- Transplant perennial, biennial, and hardy and half-hardy annual and vegetable seedlings outdoors

- Transplant shrubs, trees, ground covers, and vines

- Thin overcrowded herbs, ground covers, and perennial flowers

- Prune shade trees and summer- and autumn-flowering shrubs and trees

- Prune ground covers

- Train and prune vines

- Divide and transplant ground covers and perennial herbs and flowers

- Fertilize shrubs, trees, ground covers, vines, fruits, and perennial herbs and flowers as growth starts

- Keep the garden free of weeds

- Spray with insecticides and fungicides if needed

- Water as needed

- Root chrysanthemums

- Take stem cuttings of woody plants for rooting

- Layer stems and vines for propagating

- Disbud roses and other flowering plants for larger blooms

- Apply summer mulch

- Sow grass seed; lay sod; plant plugs

- Thatch and aerate the lawn

- Mow and edge the lawn as needed

- Fertilize the lawn for the first time if two or three feedings are needed

Zone 2

- Prepare soil for planting

- Fertilize roses and early flowering bulbs

- Divide and transplant early flowering bulbs

- Sow perennial and biennial herb and flower seeds outdoors

- Sow seeds of hardy and half-hardy annuals and vegetables outdoors

- Sow tender annual and vegetable seeds that require 4 to 6 weeks indoors

- Plant potted or bare-root roses, shrubs, trees, ground covers, vines, and perennial and biennial herbs and flowers, and B&B

shrubs, trees, ground covers, and vines

- Transplant perennial, biennial, and hardy and half-hardy annual and vegetable seedlings outdoors

- Transplant shrubs, trees, ground covers, and vines

- Prune shade trees and summer- and autumn-flowering shrubs and trees

- Prune ground covers

- Train and prune vines

- Thin overcrowded herbs, ground covers, and perennial flowers

- Divide and transplant ground covers and perennial herbs and flowers

- Fertilize shrubs, trees, ground covers, vines, fruits, and perennial herbs and flowers as growth starts

- Keep the garden free of weeds

- Spray with insecticides and fungicides if needed

- Water as needed

- Root chrysanthemums

- Take stem cuttings of woody plants for rooting

- Layer stems and vines for propagating

- Disbud roses and other flowering plants for larger blooms

- Apply summer mulch

- Sow grass seed; lay sod; plant plugs

- Thatch and aerate the lawn

- Mow and edge the lawn as needed

- Fertilize the lawn for the first time if two or three feedings are needed

Zone 3

- Prepare soil for planting

- Fertilize roses and early flowering bulbs

- Divide and transplant early flowering bulbs

- Plant summer-flowering bulbs

- Sow perennial and biennial herb and flower seeds outdoors

- Sow hardy and half-hardy annual and vegetable seeds outdoors

- Sow tender annual and vegetable seeds that require 4 to 6 weeks indoors

- Plant potted or bare-root roses, shrubs, trees, ground covers, vines, and perennial and biennial herbs and flowers, and B&B shrubs, trees, ground covers, and vines

- Transplant perennial, biennial, and hardy and half-hardy annual and vegetable seedlings outdoors

- Transplant shrubs, trees, ground covers, and vines

- Protect tender plants from unexpected frosts if needed

- Prune shade trees and summer- and autumn-flowering shrubs and trees

- Prune ground covers

- Train and prune vines

- Thin overcrowded herbs, perennial flowers, and ground covers

- Divide and transplant ground covers and perennial herbs and flowers

- Fertilize shrubs, trees, ground covers, vines, fruits, and perennial herbs and flowers as growth starts

- Keep the garden free of weeds

- Spray with insecticides and fungicides if needed

- Water as needed

- Root chrysanthemums

- Take stem cuttings of woody plants for rooting

- Layer stems and vines for propagating

- Disbud roses and other flowering plants for larger blooms

- Apply summer mulch

- Sow grass seed; lay sod; plant plugs

- Thatch and aerate the lawn

- Mow and edge the lawn as needed

- Fertilize the lawn for the first time if two or three feedings are needed

Zone 4

- Divide and transplant spring-flowering bulbs

- Fertilize bulbs and roses

- Plant summer-flowering bulbs

- Sow perennial and biennial herb and flower seeds outdoors

- Sow hardy and half-hardy annual and vegetable seeds outdoors

- Start sowing seeds outdoors for succession plantings

- Plant potted or bare-root roses, shrubs, trees, ground covers, vines, and perennial and biennial herbs and flowers, and B&B shrubs, trees, ground covers, and vines

- Transplant perennial, biennial, and hardy and half-hardy annual and vegetable seedlings outdoors

- Transplant shrubs, trees, ground covers, and vines

- Protect tender plants from unexpected frosts if needed

- Prune shade trees and summer- and autumn-flowering shrubs and trees

- Prune ground covers

- Train and prune vines

- Thin overcrowded herbs, perennial flowers, seedlings, and ground covers
- Divide and transplant ground covers and perennial herbs and flowers
- Fertilize shrubs, trees, ground covers, vines, fruits, and perennial herbs and flowers as growth starts
- Keep the garden free of weeds
- Spray with insecticides and fungicides if needed
- Water as needed
- Root chrysanthemums
- Take stem cuttings of woody plants for rooting
- Layer stems and vines for propagating
- Disbud roses and other flowering plants for larger blooms
- Apply summer mulch
- Sow grass seed; lay sod; plant plugs
- Thatch and aerate the lawn
- Mow and edge the lawn as needed
- Fertilize the lawn for the first time if two or three feedings are needed

Zone 5

- Divide and transplant spring-flowering bulbs

- Fertilize bulbs and roses
- Plant summer-flowering bulbs
- Remove faded flowers
- Remove dead bulb foliage
- Sow annual, perennial, and biennial herb, vegetable, and flower seeds outdoors
- Start sowing seeds outdoors for succession plantings
- Move seedlings outdoors
- Thin overgrown herbs, perennial flowers, seedlings, and ground covers
- Remove runners from strawberries
- Plant potted roses, shrubs, trees, ground covers, vines, herbs, and perennial flowers, and B&B shrubs, trees, ground covers, and vines
- Divide and transplant ground covers and perennial herbs and flowers
- Fertilize ground covers and perennial herbs and flowers as growth starts
- Prune shade trees and summer- and autumn-flowering shrubs and trees
- Prune spring-flowering shrubs and trees after they bloom
- Shear fine-needled evergreens as needed
- Prune ground covers

- Train and prune vines
- Keep the garden free of weeds
- Water as needed
- Spray with insecticides and fungicides if needed
- Root chrysanthemums
- Disbud roses and other flowering plants for larger blooms
- Apply summer mulch
- Take stem cuttings of woody plants for rooting
- Layer stems and vines for propagating
- Sow grass seed; lay sod; plant plugs
- Thatch and aerate the lawn
- Mow and edge the lawn as needed
- Fertilize the lawn for the first time if two or three feedings are needed

Zone 6

- Divide and transplant spring-flowering bulbs
- Fertilize bulbs and roses
- Plant summer-flowering bulbs
- Remove faded flowers
- Remove dead bulb foliage
- Sow annual, perennial, and biennial herb, vegetable, and flower seeds outdoors

- Move seedlings outdoors

- Start to sow seeds outdoors for succession plantings

- Thin overgrown herbs, perennial flowers, seedlings, and ground covers

- Remove runners from strawberries

- Plant potted roses, shrubs, trees, ground covers, vines, herbs, and perennial flowers, and B&B shrubs, trees, ground covers, and vines

- Prune shade trees and summer- and autumn-flowering shrubs and trees

- Prune spring-flowering shrubs and trees after they bloom

- Prune ground covers

- Train and prune vines

- Shear fine-needled evergreens as needed

- Divide and transplant ground covers and perennial herbs and flowers

- Fertilize ground covers and perennial herbs and flowers as growth starts

- Keep the garden free of weeds

- Water as needed

- Spray with insecticides and fungicides if needed

- Root chrysanthemums

- Disbud roses and other flowering plants for larger blooms

- Apply summer mulch

- Take stem cuttings of woody plants for rooting

- Layer stems and vines for propagating

- Sow grass seed; lay sod; plant plugs

- Thatch and aerate the lawn

- Mow and edge the lawn as needed

- Fertilize the lawn for the first time if two or three feedings are needed

Zone 7

- Divide and transplant spring-flowering bulbs

- Fertilize bulbs and roses

- Plant summer-flowering bulbs

- Remove faded flowers

- Remove dead bulb foliage

- Sow annual, perennial, and biennial herb, vegetable, and flower seeds outdoors

- Move seedlings outdoors

- Thin overgrown ground covers, herbs, seedlings, and perennial flowers

- Remove runners from strawberries

- Start to sow seeds outdoors for succession plantings

- Plant potted roses, shrubs, trees, ground covers, vines, herbs, and perennial flowers, and B&B shrubs, trees, ground covers, and vines

- Divide and transplant ground covers and perennial herbs and flowers

- Fertilize ground covers and perennial herbs and flowers as growth starts

- Prune shade trees and summer- and autumn-flowering shrubs and trees

- Prune spring-flowering shrubs and trees after they bloom

- Shear fine-needled evergreens as needed

- Prune ground covers

- Train and prune vines

- Keep the garden free of weeds

- Water as needed

- Spray with insecticides and fungicides if needed

- Root chrysanthemums

- Disbud roses and other flowering plants for larger blooms

- Apply summer mulch

- Take stem cuttings of woody plants for rooting

- Layer stems and vines for propagating

- Lay sod; plant plugs

- Mow and edge the lawn as needed

Zone 8

- Divide and transplant spring-flowering bulbs

- Continue to plant summer-flowering bulbs

- Remove faded flowers

- Remove dead bulb foliage

- Plant potted roses, shrubs, trees, ground covers, vines, herbs, and perennial flowers, and B&B shrubs, trees, ground covers, and vines

- Move seedlings outdoors

- Sow seeds outdoors for succession plantings

- Fertilize plants as needed; fertilize roses

- Prune shade trees

- Prune ground covers

- Train and prune vines

- Keep the garden free of weeds

- Harvest herb seeds and leaves

- Harvest vegetables and fruits when ripe

- Thin fruits for larger fruits

- Cut flowers for fresh use or drying

- Water as needed

- Spray with insecticides and fungicides if needed

- Apply summer mulch

- Pinch annuals and perennials as needed

- Remove runners from strawberries

- Disbud roses and other flowering plants for larger blooms

- Take stem cuttings of woody plants for rooting

- Layer stems and vines for propagating

- Lay sod; plant plugs

- Mow and edge the lawn as needed

Zone 9

- Divide and transplant spring-flowering bulbs

- Continue to plant summer-flowering bulbs

- Remove faded flowers

- Remove dead bulb foliage

- Plant potted roses, shrubs, trees, ground covers, vines, herbs, and perennial flowers, and B&B shrubs, trees, ground covers, and vines

- Add summer annuals to the garden

- Sow seeds outdoors for succession plantings

- Prune shade trees

- Prune ground covers; shear low-growing plants

- Train and prune vines

- Fertilize plants as needed; fertilize roses

- Keep the garden free of weeds

- Harvest herb seeds and leaves

- Harvest vegetables and fruits when ripe

- Thin fruits for larger fruits

- Cut flowers for fresh use or drying

- Water as needed

- Spray with insecticides and fungicides if needed

- Apply summer mulch

- Pinch annuals and perennials as needed

- Remove runners from strawberries

- Disbud roses and other flowering plants for larger blooms

- Take stem cuttings of woody plants for rooting

- Layer stems and vines for propagating

- Lay sod; plant plugs

- Mow and edge the lawn as needed

Zone 10

- Divide and transplant spring-flowering bulbs
- Continue to plant summer-flowering bulbs
- Remove faded flowers
- Remove dead bulb foliage
- Plant potted roses, shrubs, trees, ground covers, vines, herbs, and perennial flowers, and B&B shrubs, trees, ground covers, and vines
- Add summer annuals to the garden
- Sow seeds outdoors for succession plantings
- Prune shade trees
- Prune ground covers; shear low-growing plants
- Train and prune vines
- Fertilize plants as needed; fertilize roses
- Keep the garden free of weeds
- Harvest herb seeds and leaves
- Harvest vegetables and fruits when ripe
- Thin fruits for larger fruits
- Cut flowers for fresh use or drying
- Water as needed
- Spray with insecticides and fungicides if needed
- Apply summer mulch
- Pinch annuals and perennials as needed
- Remove runners from strawberries
- Disbud roses and other flowering plants for larger blooms
- Take stem cuttings of woody plants for rooting
- Layer stems and vines for propagating
- Lay sod; plant plugs
- Mow and edge the lawn as needed

Zone 11

- Divide and transplant spring-flowering bulbs
- Continue to plant summer-flowering bulbs
- Remove faded flowers
- Remove dead bulb foliage
- Plant potted roses, shrubs, trees, ground covers, vines, herbs, and perennial flowers, and B&B shrubs, trees, ground covers, and vines
- Add summer annuals to the garden

- Sow seeds outdoors for succession plantings
- Prune shade trees
- Prune ground covers; shear low-growing plants
- Train and prune vines
- Fertilize plants as needed; fertilize roses
- Keep the garden free of weeds
- Harvest herb seeds and leaves
- Harvest vegetables and fruits when ripe
- Thin fruits for larger fruits
- Cut flowers for fresh use or drying
- Water as needed
- Spray with insecticides and fungicides if needed
- Apply summer mulch
- Pinch annuals and perennials as needed
- Remove runners from strawberries
- Disbud roses and other flowering plants for larger blooms
- Take stem cuttings of woody plants for rooting
- Layer stems and vines for propagating
- Lay sod; plant plugs
- Mow and edge the lawn as needed

Summer

147

JUNE

1	2	3	4	5	6	7
8	9	10	11	12	13	14
15	16	17	18	19	20	21
22	23	24	25	26	27	28
29	30

Zone 1

- Plant summer-flowering bulbs

- Remove dead bulb foliage

- Fertilize bulbs and roses; fertilize other plants as needed

- Remove faded flowers

- Plant potted roses, shrubs, trees, ground covers, vines, herbs, and perennial flowers, and B&B shrubs, trees, ground covers, and vines

- Prune ground covers as needed

- Train and prune vines as needed

- Sow annual, biennial, and perennial seeds outdoors

- Move seedlings outdoors

- Thin seedlings

- Plant cool-season vegetables for autumn harvest

- Protect tender plants from unexpected frosts if needed

- Prune spring-flowering shrubs after they bloom

- Shear fine-needled evergreens and formal hedges

- Water as needed

- Apply summer mulch

- Spray with insecticides and fungicides if needed

- Move rooted chrysanthemums outdoors

- Disbud roses and other flowering plants for larger blooms

- Lay sod; plant plugs

- Mow and edge the lawn as needed

- Grow warm-season fruits and vegetables under glass or plastic to increase yield

Zone 2

- Plant summer-flowering bulbs

- Remove dead bulb foliage

- Fertilize bulbs and roses; fertilize other plants as needed

- Remove faded flowers

- Plant potted roses, shrubs, trees, ground covers, vines, herbs, and perennial flowers, and B&B shrubs, trees, ground covers, and vines

- Prune ground covers as needed

- Train and prune vines as needed

- Sow annual, biennial, and perennial seeds outdoors

- Move seedlings outdoors

- Plant cool-season vegetables for autumn harvest

- Thin seedlings

- Thin fruits for larger fruits

- Protect fruits from birds

- Protect tender plants from unexpected frosts if needed

- Prune spring-flowering shrubs after they bloom

- Shear fine-needled evergreens and formal hedges

- Stake tall plants

- Keep the garden free of weeds

- Water if needed

- Apply summer mulch

- Spray with insecticides and fungicides if needed

- Move rooted chrysanthemums outdoors

- Disbud roses and other flowering plants for larger blooms

- Lay sod; plant plugs

- Mow and edge the lawn as needed

- Grow warm-season fruits and vegetables under glass or plastic to increase yield

148

Zone 3

- Plant summer-flowering bulbs

- Remove dead bulb foliage

- Fertilize bulbs and roses; fertilize other plants as needed

- Remove faded flowers

- Plant potted roses, shrubs, trees, ground covers, vines, herbs, and perennial flowers, and B&B shrubs, trees, ground covers, and vines

- Prune ground covers as needed

- Train and prune vines as needed

- Sow annual, biennial, and perennial seeds outdoors

- Move seedlings outdoors

- Thin seedlings

- Thin fruits for larger fruits

- Protect fruits from birds

- Plant cool-season vegetables for autumn harvest

- Prune spring-flowering shrubs after they bloom

- Shear fine-needled evergreens and formal hedges

- Stake tall plants

- Keep the garden free of weeds

- Water as needed

- Apply summer mulch

- Spray with insecticides and fungicides if needed

- Move rooted chrysanthemums outdoors

- Disbud roses and other flowering plants for larger blooms

- Lay sod; plant plugs

- Mow and edge the lawn as needed

- Grow warm-season fruits and vegetables under glass or plastic to increase yield

Zone 4

- Remove dead bulb foliage

- Fertilize bulbs and roses; fertilize other plants as needed

- Remove faded flowers

- Plant potted roses, shrubs, trees, ground covers, vines, herbs, and perennial flowers, and B&B shrubs, trees, ground covers, and vines

- Prune ground covers as needed

- Train and prune vines as needed

- Sow annual, biennial, and perennial seeds outdoors

- Move seedlings outdoors

- Thin seedlings

- Thin fruits for larger fruits

- Protect fruits from birds

- Sow seeds outdoors for succession plantings

- Prune spring-flowering shrubs after they bloom

- Shear fine-needled evergreens and formal hedges

- Stake tall plants

- Keep the garden free of weeds

- Water as needed

- Apply summer mulch

- Spray with insecticides and fungicides if needed

- Move rooted chrysanthemum cuttings outdoors

- Disbud roses and other flowering plants for larger blooms

- Lay sod; plant plugs

- Mow and edge the lawn as needed

- Grow warm-season fruits and vegetables under glass or plastic to increase yield

Zone 5

- Remove dead bulb foliage

- Fertilize bulbs and roses; fertilize other plants as needed

- Remove faded flowers

- Plant potted roses, shrubs, trees, ground covers, vines, herbs, and perennial flowers, and B&B shrubs, trees, ground covers, and vines

- Prune ground covers as needed

- Thin seedlings

- Thin fruits for larger fruits

- Protect fruits from birds

149

- Sow seeds outdoors for succession plantings

- Train and prune vines as needed

- Prune spring-flowering shrubs after they bloom

- Shear formal hedges

- Keep the garden free of weeds

- Stake tall plants

- Harvest herb seeds and leaves

- Harvest vegetables and fruits when ripe

- Cut flowers for fresh use or drying

- Water as needed

- Apply summer mulch

- Spray with insecticides and fungicides if needed

- Move rooted chrysanthemums outdoors

- Pinch annuals and perennials as needed

- Disbud roses and other flowering plants for larger blooms

- Lay sod; plant plugs

- Mow and edge the lawn as needed

- Grow warm-season fruits and vegetables under glass or plastic in cool areas to increase yield

Zone 6

- Remove dead bulb foliage

- Fertilize bulbs and roses; fertilize other plants as needed

- Remove faded flowers

- Plant potted roses, shrubs, trees, ground covers, vines, herbs, and perennial flowers, and B&B shrubs, trees, ground covers, and vines

- Prune ground covers as needed

- Train and prune vines as needed

- Thin seedlings

- Thin grapes and other fruits for larger fruits

- Protect fruits from birds

- Sow seeds outdoors for succession plantings

- Prune spring-flowering shrubs after they bloom

- Shear formal hedges

- Keep the garden free of weeds

- Stake tall plants

- Harvest herb seeds and leaves

- Harvest vegetables and fruits when ripe

- Cut flowers for fresh use or drying

- Water as needed

- Apply summer mulch

- Spray with insecticides and fungicides if needed

- Move rooted chrysanthemums outdoors

- Pinch annuals and perennials as needed

- Disbud roses and other flowering plants for larger blooms

- Lay sod; plant plugs

- Mow and edge the lawn as needed

- Grow warm-season fruits and vegetables under glass or plastic in cool areas to increase yield

Zone 7

- Remove dead bulb foliage

- Fertilize bulbs and roses; fertilize other plants as needed

- Remove faded flowers

- Plant potted roses, shrubs, trees, ground covers, vines, herbs, and perennial flowers, and B&B shrubs, trees, ground covers, and vines

- Prune ground covers as needed

- Train and prune vines as needed

- Prune spring-flowering shrubs after they bloom

- Thin seedlings

- Thin grapes and other fruits for larger fruits

- Protect fruits from birds

- Sow seeds outdoors for succession plantings

- Shear formal hedges

- Keep the garden free of weeds

- Stake tall plants

- Harvest herb seeds and leaves

- Harvest vegetables and fruits when ripe

- Cut flowers for fresh use or drying

- Water as needed

- Apply summer mulch

- Spray with insecticides and fungicides if needed

- Move rooted chrysanthemums outdoors

- Pinch annuals and perennials as needed

- Disbud roses and other flowering plants for larger blooms

- Lay sod; plant plugs

- Mow and edge the lawn as needed

- Grow warm-season fruits and vegetables under glass or plastic in cool areas to increase yield

Zone 8

- Remove dead bulb foliage

- Fertilize bulbs and roses; fertilize other plants as needed

- Remove faded flowers

- Plant potted roses, shrubs, trees, ground covers, vines, herbs, and perennial flowers, and B&B shrubs, trees, ground covers, and vines

- Sow seeds outdoors for succession plantings

- Prune ground covers as needed; shear low-growing plants

- Train and prune vines as needed

- Shear formal hedges

- Keep the garden free of weeds

- Harvest herb seeds and leaves

- Harvest vegetables and fruits when ripe

- Cut flowers for fresh use or drying

- Water as needed

- Spray with insecticides and fungicides if needed

- Pinch annuals and perennials as needed

- Thin grapes and other fruits for larger fruits

- Protect fruits from birds

- Disbud roses and other flowering plants for larger blooms

- Lay sod; plant plugs

- Mow and edge the lawn as needed

Zone 9

- Remove dead bulb foliage

- Fertilize bulbs and roses; fertilize other plants as needed

- Remove faded flowers

- Plant potted roses, shrubs, trees, ground covers, vines, herbs, and perennial flowers, and B&B shrubs, trees, ground covers, and vines

- Prune ground covers as needed; shear low-growing plants

- Train and prune vines as needed

- Shear formal hedges

- Keep the garden free of weeds

- Harvest herb seeds and leaves

- Harvest vegetables and fruits when ripe

- Thin grapes and other fruits for larger fruits

- Protect fruits from birds

- Cut flowers for fresh use or drying

- Water as needed

151

- Spray with insecticides and fungicides if needed

- Pinch annuals and perennials as needed

- Disbud roses and other flowering plants for larger blooms

- Remove hardy and half-hardy annuals and vegetables as they fade

- Lay sod; plant plugs

- Mow and edge the lawn as needed

Zone 10

- Remove dead bulb foliage

- Fertilize bulbs and roses; fertilize other plants as needed

- Remove faded flowers

- Plant potted roses, shrubs, trees, ground covers, vines, herbs, and perennial flowers, and B&B shrubs, trees, ground covers, and vines

- Prune ground covers as needed; shear low-growing plants

- Train and prune vines as needed

- Shear formal hedges

- Keep the garden free of weeds

- Harvest herb seeds and leaves

- Harvest vegetables and fruits when ripe

- Thin fruits for larger fruits

- Protect fruits from birds

- Cut flowers for fresh use or drying

- Water as needed

- Spray with insecticides and fungicides if needed

- Pinch annuals and perennials as needed

- Disbud roses and other flowering plants for larger blooms

- Remove hardy and half-hardy annuals and vegetables as they fade

- Lay sod; plant plugs

- Mow and edge the lawn as needed

Zone 11

- Remove dead bulb foliage

- Fertilize bulbs and roses; fertilize other plants as needed

- Remove faded flowers

- Plant potted roses, shrubs, trees, ground covers, vines, herbs, and perennial flowers, and B&B shrubs, trees, ground covers, and vines

- Prune ground covers as needed; shear low-growing plants

- Train and prune vines as needed

- Shear formal hedges

- Keep the garden free of weeds

- Harvest herb seeds and leaves

- Harvest vegetables and fruits when ripe

- Thin fruits for larger fruits

- Protect fruits from birds

- Cut flowers for fresh use or drying

- Water as needed

- Spray with insecticides and fungicides if needed

- Pinch annuals and perennials as needed

- Disbud roses and other flowering plants for larger blooms

- Remove hardy and half-hardy annuals and vegetables as they fade

- Lay sod; plant plugs

- Mow and edge the lawn as needed

J U L Y

1	2	3	4	5	6	7
8	9	10	11	12	13	14
15	16	17	18	19	20	21
22	23	24	25	26	27	28
29	30	31				

Zone 1

- Order spring-flowering bulbs
- Plant potted roses, shrubs, trees, ground covers, and perennial and biennial herbs and flowers, and B&B shrubs, trees, ground covers, and vines
- Sow perennial and biennial herb and flower seeds outdoors
- Fertilize plants as needed
- Keep the garden free of weeds
- Remove faded flowers
- Shear low-growing plants
- Pinch annuals and perennials until midmonth
- Prune ground covers; trim edges
- Train and prune vines as needed
- Disbud roses and other flowering plants for larger blooms
- Harvest herb seeds and leaves
- Harvest vegetables and fruits when ripe
- Cut flowers for fresh use or drying
- Stake tall plants
- Water as needed
- Spray with insecticides and fungicides if needed
- Take softwood cuttings for rooting
- Lay sod
- Mow and edge the lawn as needed

Zone 2

- Order spring-flowering bulbs
- Plant potted roses, shrubs, trees, ground covers, vines, and perennial and biennial herbs and flowers, and B&B shrubs, trees, ground covers, and vines
- Sow perennial and biennial herb and flower seeds outdoors
- Fertilize plants as needed
- Keep the garden free of weeds
- Remove faded flowers
- Shear low-growing plants
- Pinch annuals and perennials until midmonth
- Prune ground covers; trim edges
- Train and prune vines as needed
- Disbud roses and other flowering plants for larger blooms
- Harvest herb seeds and leaves
- Harvest vegetables and fruits when ripe
- Cut flowers for fresh use or drying
- Stake tall plants
- Water as needed
- Spray with insecticides and fungicides if needed
- Take softwood cuttings for rooting
- Lay sod
- Mow and edge the lawn as needed

Zone 3

- Order spring-flowering bulbs
- Plant potted roses, shrubs, trees, ground covers, vines, and perennial and biennial herbs and flowers, and B&B shrubs, trees, ground covers, and vines
- Sow perennial and biennial herb and flower seeds outdoors
- Fertilize plants as needed
- Keep the garden free of weeds
- Remove faded flowers
- Shear low-growing plants
- Pinch annuals and perennials until midmonth
- Prune ground covers; trim edges

153

- Train and prune vines as needed

- Disbud roses and other flowering plants for larger blooms

- Harvest herb seeds and leaves

- Harvest vegetables and fruits when ripe

- Cut flowers for fresh use or drying

- Stake tall plants

- Water as needed

- Spray with insecticides and fungicides if needed

- Take softwood cuttings for rooting

- Lay sod

- Mow and edge the lawn as needed

Zone 4

- Order spring-flowering bulbs

- Plant potted roses, shrubs, trees, ground covers, vines, and perennial and biennial herbs and flowers, and B&B shrubs, trees, ground covers, and vines

- Sow perennial and biennial herb and flower seeds outdoors

- Sow seeds outdoors for succession plantings

- Plant cool-season vegetables for autumn harvest

- Fertilize plants as needed

- Keep the garden free of weeds

- Remove faded flowers

- Shear low-growing plants

- Pinch annuals and perennials until midmonth

- Prune ground covers; trim edges

- Train and prune vines as needed

- Disbud roses and other flowering plants for larger blooms

- Harvest herb seeds and leaves

- Harvest vegetables and fruits when ripe

- Cut flowers for fresh use or drying

- Stake tall plants

- Water as needed

- Spray with insecticides and fungicides if needed

- Take softwood cuttings for rooting

- Lay sod

- Mow and edge the lawn as needed

Zone 5

- Order spring-flowering bulbs

- Plant potted roses, shrubs, trees, ground covers, vines, and perennial and biennial herbs and flowers, and B&B shrubs, trees, ground covers, and vines

- Sow perennial and biennial herb and flower seeds outdoors

- Sow seeds outdoors for succession plantings

- Plant cool-season vegetables for autumn harvest

- Keep the garden free of weeds

- Fertilize plants as needed

- Remove faded flowers

- Shear low-growing plants

- Pinch annuals and perennials until midmonth

- Prune ground covers; trim edges

- Train and prune vines as needed

- Disbud roses and other flowering plants for larger blooms

- Harvest herb seeds and leaves

- Harvest vegetables and fruits when ripe

- Cut flowers for fresh use or drying

- Stake tall plants

- Water as needed

- Spray with insecticides and fungicides if needed

154

- Take softwood cuttings for rooting
- Lay sod
- Mow and edge the lawn as needed

Zone 6

- Order spring-flowering bulbs
- Plant potted roses, shrubs, trees, ground covers, vines, and perennial and biennial herbs and flowers, and B&B shrubs, trees, ground covers, and vines
- Sow perennial and biennial herb and flower seeds outdoors
- Sow seeds outdoors for succession plantings
- Keep the garden free of weeds
- Fertilize plants as needed
- Remove faded flowers
- Shear low-growing plants
- Pinch annuals and perennials until midmonth
- Prune ground covers; trim edges
- Train and prune vines as needed
- Disbud roses and other flowering plants for larger blooms
- Harvest herb seeds and leaves
- Harvest vegetables and fruits when ripe
- Cut flowers for fresh use or drying

- Stake tall plants
- Water as needed
- Spray with insecticides and fungicides if needed
- Take softwood cuttings for rooting
- Lay sod
- Mow and edge the lawn as needed

Zone 7

- Order spring-flowering bulbs
- Plant potted roses, shrubs, trees, ground covers, vines, and perennial and biennial herbs and flowers, and B&B shrubs, trees, ground covers, and vines
- Sow perennial and biennial herb and flower seeds outdoors
- Sow seeds for succession plantings
- Keep the garden free of weeds
- Fertilize plants as needed
- Remove faded flowers
- Shear low-growing plants
- Pinch annuals and perennials until midmonth
- Prune ground covers; trim edges
- Train and prune vines as needed
- Disbud roses and other flowering plants for larger blooms
- Harvest herb seeds and leaves

- Harvest vegetables and fruits when ripe
- Cut flowers for fresh use or drying
- Stake tall plants
- Water as needed
- Spray with insecticides and fungicides if needed
- Take softwood cuttings for rooting
- Lay sod
- Mow and edge the lawn as needed

Zone 8

- Order spring-flowering bulbs
- Plant potted roses, shrubs, trees, ground covers, vines, and perennial and biennial herbs and flowers, and B&B shrubs, trees, ground covers, and vines
- Sow seeds outdoors for succession plantings
- Keep the garden free of weeds
- Fertilize as needed
- Remove faded flowers
- Pinch annuals and perennials until midmonth
- Prune ground covers; trim edges
- Train and prune vines as needed
- Disbud roses and other flowering plants for larger blooms

155

- Shear low-growing plants

- Harvest herb seeds and leaves

- Harvest vegetables and fruits when ripe

- Cut flowers for fresh use or drying

- Stake tall plants

- Water as needed

- Spray with insecticides and fungicides if needed

- Take softwood cuttings for rooting

- Lay sod

- Mow and edge the lawn as needed

- Order spring-flowering bulbs

- Plant potted roses, shrubs, trees, ground covers, vines, and perennial and biennial herbs, and B&B shrubs, trees, ground covers, and vines

- Keep the garden free of weeds

- Fertilize plants as needed

- Remove faded flowers

- Pinch annuals and perennials as needed

- Prune ground covers; trim edges

- Train and prune vines as needed

- Disbud roses and other flowering plants for larger blooms

- Shear low-growing plants

- Harvest herb seeds and leaves

- Harvest vegetables and fruits when ripe

- Cut flowers for fresh use or drying

- Stake tall plants

- Water as needed

- Spray with insecticides and fungicides if needed

- Take softwood cuttings for rooting

- Lay sod

- Mow and edge the lawn as needed

- Order spring-flowering bulbs

- Plant potted roses, shrubs, trees, ground covers, vines, and perennial and biennial herbs, and B&B shrubs, trees, ground covers, and vines

- Keep the garden free of weeds

- Fertilize plants as needed

- Remove faded flowers

- Pinch annuals and perennials as needed

- Prune ground covers; trim edges

- Train and prune vines as needed

- Disbud roses and other flowering plants for larger blooms

- Shear low-growing plants

- Harvest herb seeds and leaves

- Harvest vegetables and fruits when ripe

- Cut flowers for fresh use or drying

- Stake tall plants

- Water as needed

- Spray with insecticides and fungicides if needed

- Take softwood cuttings for rooting

- Lay sod

- Mow and edge the lawn as needed

Zone 11

- Order spring-flowering bulbs

- Plant potted roses, shrubs, trees, ground covers, vines, and perennial and biennial herbs, and B&B shrubs, trees, ground covers, and vines

- Keep the garden free of weeds

- Fertilize plants as needed

- Remove faded flowers

- Pinch annuals and perennials as needed

- Prune ground covers; trim edges

- Train and prune vines as needed

- Disbud roses and other flowering plants for larger blooms

- Shear low-growing plants

- Harvest herb seeds and leaves

- Harvest vegetables and fruits when ripe

- Cut flowers for fresh use or drying

- Stake tall plants

- Water as needed

- Spray with insecticides and fungicides if needed

- Take softwood cuttings for rooting

- Lay sod

- Mow and edge the lawn as needed

AUGUST

1	2	3	4	5	6	7
8	9	10	11	12	13	14
15	16	17	18	19	20	21
22	23	24	25	26	27	28
29	30	31				

Zone 1

- Plant autumn-flowering bulbs

- Plant potted roses, shrubs, trees, ground covers, vines, and perennial and biennial herbs and flowers, and B&B shrubs, trees, ground covers, and vines

- Transplant evergreens

- Prune ground covers if needed; trim low-growing plants

- Train and prune vines

- Fertilize plants, if needed, for the last time until dormancy

- Keep the garden free of weeds

- Water as needed

- Spray with insecticides and fungicides if needed

- Remove faded flowers

- Harvest herb seeds and leaves

- Harvest vegetables and fruits when ripe

- Cut flowers for fresh use or drying

- Lay sod

- Mow and edge the lawn as needed

- Aerate the lawn if needed

Zone 2

- Plant autumn-flowering bulbs

- Plant potted roses, shrubs, trees, ground covers, vines, and perennial and biennial herbs and flowers, and B&B shrubs, trees, ground covers, and vines

- Transplant evergreens

- Prune ground covers if needed; trim low-growing plants

- Train and prune vines

- Fertilize plants, if needed, for the last time until dormancy

- Keep the garden free of weeds

- Water as needed

- Spray with insecticides and fungicides if needed

- Remove faded flowers

- Harvest herb seeds and leaves

- Harvest vegetables and fruits when ripe

- Cut flowers for fresh use or drying

- Lay sod

157

- Mow and edge the lawn as needed
- Aerate the lawn if needed

Zone 3

- Plant autumn-flowering bulbs
- Plant potted roses, shrubs, trees, ground covers, vines, and perennial and biennial herbs and flowers, and B&B shrubs, trees, ground covers, and vines
- Plant irises, poppies, and peonies
- Transplant evergreens
- Prune ground covers if needed; trim low-growing plants
- Train and prune vines
- Fertilize plants, if needed, for the last time until dormancy
- Keep the garden free of weeds
- Water as needed
- Spray with insecticides and fungicides if needed
- Remove faded flowers
- Harvest herb seeds and leaves
- Harvest vegetables and fruits when ripe
- Cut flowers for fresh use or drying
- Lay sod
- Mow and edge the lawn as needed
- Aerate the lawn if needed

Zone 4

- Plant autumn-flowering bulbs
- Plant potted roses, shrubs, trees, ground covers, vines, and perennial and biennial herbs and flowers, and B&B shrubs, trees, ground covers, and vines
- Plant irises, poppies, and peonies
- Prune ground covers if needed; trim low-growing plants
- Train and prune vines
- Fertilize plants, if needed, for the last time until dormancy
- Keep the garden free of weeds
- Water as needed
- Spray with insecticides and fungicides if needed
- Remove faded flowers
- Harvest herb seeds and leaves
- Harvest vegetables and fruits when ripe
- Sow vegetable seeds outdoors for succession plantings
- Cut flowers for fresh use or drying
- Lay sod
- Mow and edge the lawn
- Aerate the lawn if needed

Zone 5

- Order spring-flowering bulbs
- Plant autumn-flowering bulbs
- Plant potted roses, shrubs, trees, ground covers, vines, and perennial and biennial herbs and flowers, and B&B shrubs, trees, ground covers, and vines
- Prune ground covers if needed; trim low-growing plants
- Train and prune vines
- Fertilize plants, if needed, for the last time until dormancy
- Keep the garden free of weeds
- Water as needed
- Spray with insecticides and fungicides if needed
- Remove faded flowers
- Harvest herb seeds and leaves
- Harvest vegetables and fruits when ripe
- Sow vegetable seeds outdoors for succession plantings
- Remove runners from strawberries
- Cut flowers for fresh use or drying
- Pinch leggy plants
- Sow hardy and half-hardy annual seeds indoors or outdoors
- Lay sod
- Mow and edge the lawn as needed
- Aerate the lawn if needed

Zone 6

- Order spring-flowering bulbs

- Plant autumn-flowering bulbs

- Plant potted roses, shrubs, trees, ground covers, vines, and perennial and biennial herbs and flowers, and B&B shrubs, trees, ground covers, and vines

- Prune ground covers if needed; trim low-growing plants

- Train and prune vines

- Fertilize plants, if needed, for the last time until dormancy

- Keep the garden free of weeds

- Water as needed

- Spray with insecticides and fungicides if needed

- Remove faded flowers

- Harvest herb seeds and leaves

- Harvest vegetables and fruits when ripe

- Remove runners from strawberries

- Plant cool-season vegetables for autumn harvest

- Sow vegetable seeds outdoors for succession plantings

- Cut flowers for fresh use or drying

- Pinch leggy plants

- Sow hardy and half-hardy annual seeds indoors or outdoors

- Lay sod

- Mow and edge the lawn as needed

- Aerate the lawn if needed

Zone 7

- Order spring-flowering bulbs

- Plant autumn-flowering bulbs

- Plant potted roses, shrubs, trees, ground covers, vines, and perennial and biennial herbs and flowers, and B&B trees, shrubs, ground covers, and vines

- Prune ground covers if needed; trim low-growing plants

- Train and prune vines

- Fertilize plants, if needed, for the last time until dormancy

- Keep the garden free of weeds

- Water as needed

- Spray with insecticides and fungicides if needed

- Remove faded flowers

- Harvest herb seeds and leaves

- Harvest vegetables and fruits when ripe

- Remove runners from strawberries

- Plant cool-season vegetables for autumn harvest

- Sow vegetable seeds outdoors for succession plantings

- Cut flowers for fresh use or drying

- Pinch leggy plants

- Sow hardy and half-hardy annual seeds indoors or outdoors

- Lay sod

- Mow and edge the lawn as needed

- Aerate the lawn if needed

Zone 8

- Order spring-flowering bulbs

- Plant autumn-flowering bulbs

- Plant potted roses, shrubs, trees, ground covers, vines, and perennial and biennial herbs and flowers, and B&B shrubs, trees, ground covers, and vines

- Prune ground covers if needed; trim low-growing plants

- Train and prune vines

- Fertilize roses; fertilize other plants if needed

- Keep the garden free of weeds

- Water as needed

- Spray with insecticides and fungicides if needed

- Disbud roses and other flowering plants for larger blooms

- Remove faded flowers

- Harvest herb seeds and leaves

- Harvest vegetables and fruits when ripe

159

- ◆ Train and prune vines

- ◆ Fertilize roses; fertilize other plants if needed

- ◆ Keep the garden free of weeds

- ◆ Water as needed

- ◆ Spray with insecticides and fungicides if needed

- ◆ Pinch annuals and perennials if needed

- ◆ Disbud roses and other flowering plants for larger blooms

- ◆ Remove faded flowers

- ◆ Harvest herb seeds and leaves

- ◆ Harvest vegetables and fruits when ripe

- ◆ Remove runners from strawberries

- ◆ Cut flowers for fresh use or drying

- ◆ Replace spent annual flowers

- ◆ Sow hardy and half-hardy annual seeds indoors or outdoors

- ◆ Lay sod

- ◆ Mow and edge the lawn as needed

- ◆ Remove runners from strawberries

- ◆ Plant cool-season vegetables for autumn harvest

- ◆ Sow vegetable seeds outdoors for succession plantings

- ◆ Cut flowers for fresh use or drying

- ◆ Pinch leggy plants

- ◆ Sow hardy and half-hardy annual seeds indoors or outdoors

- ◆ Lay sod

- ◆ Mow and edge the lawn as needed

- ◆ Aerate the lawn if needed

Zone 9

- ◆ Plant autumn-flowering bulbs

- ◆ Plant potted roses, shrubs, trees, ground covers, vines, and perennial and biennial herbs and flowers, and B&B shrubs, trees, ground covers, and vines

- ◆ Prune ground covers if needed; trim low-growing plants

Zone 10

- ◆ Plant autumn-flowering bulbs

- ◆ Plant potted roses, shrubs, trees, ground covers, vines, and perennial and biennial herbs

160

and flowers, and B&B shrubs, trees, ground covers, and vines

- Prune ground covers if needed; trim low-growing plants

- Train and prune vines

- Fertilize roses; fertilize other plants if needed

- Keep the garden free of weeds

- Water as needed

- Spray with insecticides and fungicides if needed

- Pinch annuals and perennials if needed

- Disbud roses and other flowering plants for larger blooms

- Remove faded flowers

- Harvest herb seeds and leaves

- Harvest vegetables and fruits when ripe

- Remove runners from strawberries

- Cut flowers for fresh use or drying

- Remove and replace spent annual flowers

- Sow hardy and half-hardy annual seeds indoors or outdoors

- Lay sod

- Mow and edge the lawn as needed

Zone 11

- Plant autumn-flowering bulbs

- Plant potted roses, shrubs, trees, ground covers, vines, and perennial and biennial herbs and flowers, and B&B shrubs, trees, ground covers, and vines

- Prune ground covers if needed; trim low-growing plants

- Train and prune vines

- Fertilize roses; fertilize other plants if needed

- Keep the garden free of weeds

- Water as needed

- Spray with insecticides and fungicides if needed

- Pinch annuals and perennials if needed

- Disbud roses and other flowering plants for larger blooms

- Remove faded flowers

- Harvest herb seeds and leaves

- Harvest vegetables and fruits when ripe

- Remove runners from strawberries

- Cut flowers for fresh use or drying

- Remove and replace spent annual flowers

- Sow hardy and half-hardy annual seeds indoors or outdoors

- Lay sod

- Mow and edge the lawn as needed

161

Autumn

SEPTEMBER

1	2	3	4	5	6	7
8	9	10	11	12	13	14
15	16	17	18	19	20	21
22	23	24	25	26	27	28
29	30

Zone 1

- Prepare soil for autumn or spring planting
- Plant spring-flowering bulbs
- Dig and store tender bulbs
- Transplant deciduous shrubs and trees
- Clean up fallen leaves
- Cut back spent biennial and perennial herbs and flowers
- Remove annual flowers, vegetables, and herbs killed by frost
- Harvest herb roots and stems
- Harvest herb leaves and seeds
- Harvest vegetables and fruits when ripe
- Stop cutting roses and other flowers
- Sow seeds of woody plants and perennials needing stratification outdoors
- Apply winter protection
- Water as needed
- Repair and paint trellises, arbors, fences, benches, and garden accessories
- Sow grass seed; lay sod; plant plugs
- Mow and edge the lawn as needed
- Thatch and aerate the lawn if needed
- Fertilize the lawn for the second time if three yearly applications are needed

Zone 2

- Prepare soil for autumn or spring planting
- Plant spring-flowering bulbs
- Dig and store tender bulbs
- Transplant deciduous shrubs and trees
- Rake and clean up fallen leaves
- Cut back spent biennial and perennial herbs and flowers
- Remove annual flowers, vegetables, and herbs killed by frost
- Harvest herb roots and stems
- Harvest herb leaves and seeds
- Harvest vegetables and fruits when ripe
- Stop cutting roses and other flowers
- Sow seeds of woody plants and perennials needing stratification outdoors
- Apply winter protection
- Water as needed
- Repair and paint trellises, arbors, fences, benches, and garden accessories
- Sow grass seed; lay sod; plant plugs
- Mow and edge the lawn as needed
- Thatch and aerate the lawn if needed
- Fertilize the lawn for the second time if three yearly applications are needed

Zone 3

- Prepare soil for autumn or spring planting
- Plant spring-flowering bulbs
- Dig and store tender bulbs
- Transplant deciduous shrubs and trees
- Clean up fallen leaves
- Cut back spent biennial and perennial herbs and flowers
- Remove annual flowers, vegetables, and herbs killed by frost

163

- Harvest herb roots and stems

- Harvest herb leaves and seeds

- Harvest vegetables and fruits when ripe

- Prune raspberries

- Stop cutting roses and other flowers

- Sow seeds of woody plants and perennials needing stratification outdoors

- Apply winter protection

- Water as needed

- Repair and paint trellises, arbors, fences, benches, and garden accessories

- Sow grass seed; lay sod; plant plugs

- Mow and edge the lawn as needed

- Thatch and aerate the lawn if needed

- Fertilize the lawn for the second time if three yearly applications are needed

Zone 4

- Prepare soil for autumn or spring planting

- Plant spring-flowering bulbs

- Dig and store tender bulbs

- Transplant deciduous shrubs and trees

- Clean up fallen leaves

- Cut back spent biennial and perennial herbs and flowers

- Remove annual flowers, vegetables, and herbs killed by frost

- Harvest herb roots, stems, leaves, and seeds

- Harvest vegetables and fruits when ripe

- Prune raspberries and blackberries

- Stop cutting roses and other flowers

- Sow seeds of woody plants and perennials needing stratification outdoors

- Apply winter protection

- Water as needed

- Repair and paint trellises, arbors, fences, benches, and garden accessories

- Sow grass seed; lay sod; plant plugs

- Mow and edge the lawn as needed

- Thatch and aerate the lawn if needed

- Fertilize the lawn for the second time if three yearly applications are needed

Zone 5

- Prepare soil for autumn or spring planting

- Plant spring-flowering bulbs

- Dig and store tender bulbs

- Keep the garden free of weeds

- Sow perennial and biennial herb and flower seeds outdoors

- Divide and transplant perennial herbs and flowers

- Transplant deciduous or evergreen shrubs and trees

- Plant irises, peonies, and poppies

- Sow seeds of woody plants and perennials needing stratification outdoors

- Sow vegetable seeds outdoors for succession plantings

- Apply winter protection

- Water as needed

- Harvest herb leaves and seeds

- Harvest vegetables and fruits when ripe

- Prune raspberries, blackberries, and black currants

- Stop cutting roses and other flowers

- Remove faded flowers

- Sow grass seed; lay sod; plant plugs

- Mow and edge the lawn as needed

- Thatch and aerate the lawn if needed

- Fertilize the lawn for the second time if three yearly applications are needed

Zone 6

- Prepare soil for autumn or spring planting

- Plant spring-flowering bulbs

- Keep the garden free of weeds

- Sow perennial and biennial herb and flower seeds outdoors

- Sow vegetable seeds outdoors for succession plantings

- Divide and transplant perennial herbs and flowers

- Trim plants if needed

- Train and tie vines if needed

- Transplant evergreens

- Plant irises, poppies, and peonies

- Water as needed

- Spray with insecticides and fungicides if needed

- Harvest herb leaves and seeds

- Harvest vegetables and fruits when ripe

- Prune raspberries, blackberries, and black currants

- Cut flowers for fresh use or drying

- Remove faded flowers

- Sow grass seed; lay sod; plant plugs

- Mow and edge the lawn as needed

- Thatch and aerate the lawn if needed

- Fertilize the lawn for the second time if three yearly applications are needed

Zone 7

- Prepare soil for autumn or spring planting

- Plant spring-flowering bulbs

- Keep the garden free of weeds

- Sow perennial and biennial herb and flower seeds outdoors

- Sow vegetable seeds outdoors for succession plantings

- Divide and transplant perennial herbs and flowers

- Trim plants if needed

- Train and tie vines if needed

- Plant potted roses, shrubs, trees, ground covers, vines, and perennial herbs and flowers, and B&B shrubs, trees, ground covers, and vines

- Plant irises, poppies, and peonies

- Transplant evergreens

- Water as needed

- Spray with insecticides and fungicides if needed

- Harvest herb leaves and seeds

- Harvest vegetables and fruits when ripe

- Prune raspberries, blackberries, and black currants

- Cut flowers for fresh use or drying

- Remove faded flowers

- Take hardwood cuttings of woody plants for rooting

- Sow grass seed; lay sod; plant plugs

- Mow and edge the lawn as needed

- Thatch and aerate the lawn if needed

- Fertilize the lawn for the second time if three yearly applications are needed

Zone 8

- Prepare soil for autumn or spring planting

- Plant spring-flowering bulbs

- Keep the garden free of weeds

- Sow perennial and biennial herb and flower seeds outdoors

165

- Sow vegetable seeds outdoors for succession plantings

- Divide and transplant perennial herbs and flowers

- Plant potted roses, shrubs, trees, ground covers, vines, and perennial herbs and flowers, and B&B shrubs, trees, ground covers, and vines

- Plant irises, poppies, and peonies

- Trim plants if needed

- Train and tie vines if needed

- Transplant evergreens

- Apply final fertilizer to plants until dormancy

- Water as needed

- Spray with insecticides and fungicides if needed

- Harvest herb leaves and seeds

- Harvest vegetables and fruits when ripe

- Prune raspberries, blackberries, and black currants

- Cut flowers for fresh use or drying

- Take hardwood cuttings of woody plants for rooting

- Sow grass seed; lay sod; plant plugs

- Mow and edge the lawn as needed

- Thatch and aerate the lawn if needed

- Fertilize the lawn for the second time if three yearly applications are needed

Zone 9

- Keep the garden free of weeds

- Sow annual, perennial, and biennial herb and flower seeds outdoors

- Divide and transplant perennial herbs and flowers

- Plant potted roses, shrubs, trees, ground covers, vines, and perennial herbs and flowers, and B&B shrubs, trees, ground covers, and vines

- Trim plants if needed

- Train and tie vines if needed

- Transplant evergreens

- Water as needed

- Fertilize plants if needed

- Spray with insecticides and fungicides if needed

- Harvest herb leaves and seeds

- Harvest vegetables and fruits when ripe

- Prune blackberries

- Plant cool-season vegetables for autumn harvest

- Sow hardy and half-hardy annual and vegetable seeds indoors

- Cut flowers for fresh use or drying

- Remove faded flowers

- Take hardwood cuttings of woody plants for rooting

- Lay sod; plant plugs

- Mow and edge the lawn as needed

- Thatch and aerate the lawn if needed

- Fertilize the lawn for the second time if three yearly applications are needed

Zone 10

- Keep the garden free of weeds

- Sow annual, perennial, and biennial herb and flower seeds outdoors

- Divide and transplant perennial herbs and flowers

- Plant potted roses, shrubs, trees, ground covers, vines, and perennial herbs and flowers, and B&B shrubs, trees, ground covers, and vines

- Trim plants if needed

- Train and tie vines if needed

- Transplant evergreens

- Water as needed

- Fertilize plants if needed

- Spray with insecticides and fungicides if needed

- Harvest herb leaves and seeds

- Harvest vegetables and fruits when ripe

- Plant cool-season vegetables for autumn harvest

- Sow hardy and half-hardy annual and vegetable seeds indoors

- Cut flowers for fresh use or drying

- Remove faded flowers

- Lay sod; plant plugs

- Mow and edge the lawn as needed

- Thatch and aerate the lawn if needed

- Fertilize the lawn for the second time if three yearly applications are needed

Zone 11

- Keep the garden free of weeds

- Sow annual, perennial, and biennial herb and flower seeds outdoors

- Divide and transplant perennial herbs and flowers

- Plant potted roses, shrubs, trees, ground covers, vines, and perennial herbs and flowers, and B&B shrubs, trees, ground covers, and vines

- Trim plants if needed

- Train and tie vines if needed

- Transplant evergreens

- Water as needed

- Fertilize plants if needed

- Spray with insecticides and fungicides if needed

- Harvest herb leaves and seeds

- Harvest vegetables and fruits when ripe

- Plant cool-season vegetables for autumn harvest

- Sow hardy and half-hardy annual and vegetable seeds indoors

- Cut flowers for fresh use or drying

- Remove faded flowers

- Lay sod; plant plugs

- Mow and edge the lawn as needed

- Thatch and aerate the lawn if needed

- Fertilize the lawn for the second time if three yearly applications are needed

O C T O B E R

1	2	3	4	5	6	7
8	9	10	11	12	13	14
15	16	17	18	19	20	21
22	23	24	25	26	27	28
29	30	31				

Zone 1

- Pot bulbs for forcing and begin to chill them

- Apply winter protection

- Apply dormant fertilizer to trees, shrubs, ground covers, and vines

- Prune shade trees

- Rake leaves

- Spray evergreens with antidesiccant

- Mow and edge the lawn if needed

- Fertilize the lawn if one feeding is needed, if not done in the spring

- Fertilize the lawn for the second time if two yearly feedings are needed or for the third time if three yearly feedings are needed

167

Zone 2

- Pot bulbs for forcing and begin to chill them
- Apply winter protection
- Apply dormant fertilizer to trees, shrubs, ground covers, and vines
- Prune shade trees
- Rake leaves
- Spray evergreens with antidesiccant
- Mow and edge the lawn if needed
- Fertilize the lawn if one feeding is needed, if not done in the spring
- Fertilize the lawn for the second time if two yearly feedings are needed or for the third time if three yearly feedings are needed

Zone 3

- Pot bulbs for forcing and begin to chill them
- Apply winter protection
- Apply dormant fertilizer to trees, shrubs, ground covers, and vines
- Remove annual flowers, herbs, and vegetables killed by frost
- Prune shade trees
- Rake leaves

- Spray evergreens with antidesiccant
- Repair and paint trellises, arbors, fences, benches, and garden accessories
- Mow and edge the lawn if needed
- Fertilize the lawn if one feeding is needed, if not done in the spring
- Fertilize the lawn for the second time if two yearly feedings are needed or for the third time if three yearly feedings are needed

Zone 4

- Pot bulbs for forcing and begin to chill them
- Apply winter protection
- Apply dormant fertilizer to trees, shrubs, ground covers, and vines
- Remove annual flowers, herbs, and vegetables killed by frost
- Plant very hardy annuals
- Prune shade trees
- Rake leaves
- Spray evergreens with antidesiccant
- Repair and paint trellises, arbors, fences, benches, and garden accessories
- Mow and edge the lawn if needed

- Fertilize the lawn if one feeding is needed, if not done in the spring
- Fertilize the lawn for the second time if two yearly feedings are needed or for the third time if three yearly feedings are needed

Zone 5

- Prepare soil for spring planting
- Water as needed
- Remove annuals killed by frost
- Plant hardy annuals
- Transplant roses, deciduous trees and shrubs, and ground covers
- Prune shade trees
- Rake leaves
- Harvest herb roots and stems
- Harvest herb leaves and seeds
- Harvest vegetables and fruits when ripe
- Cut flowers for fresh use or drying
- Pot bulbs for forcing and begin to chill them
- Repair and paint trellises, arbors, fences, benches, and garden accessories
- Mow and edge the lawn if needed

168

Zone 6

- Prepare soil for spring planting
- Keep the garden free of weeds
- Plant potted perennial and biennial herbs and flowers
- Plant bare-root trees, shrubs, ground covers, and vines
- Divide and transplant perennial herbs and flowers and ground covers
- Transplant deciduous trees and shrubs
- Plant hardy annuals
- Prune shade trees
- Rake leaves
- Harvest herb roots and stems
- Harvest herb leaves and seeds
- Harvest vegetables and fruits when ripe
- Sow seeds outdoors for succession plantings
- Cut flowers for fresh use or drying
- Pot bulbs for forcing and begin to chill them
- Plant spring-flowering bulbs
- Dig and store tender bulbs
- Water plants if needed, especially evergreens
- Sow seeds of woody plants and perennials that need stratification outdoors

- Repair and paint trellises, arbors, fences, benches, and garden accessories
- Mow and edge the lawn if needed

Zone 7

- Prepare soil for spring planting
- Keep the garden free of weeds
- Plant potted perennial and biennial herbs and flowers, roses, trees, shrubs, ground covers, and vines, and B&B trees, shrubs, ground covers, and vines
- Divide and transplant perennial herbs and flowers and ground covers
- Plant bare-root shrubs, trees, ground covers, and vines
- Transplant deciduous trees and shrubs
- Plant hardy annuals
- Water as needed
- Spray with insecticides and fungicides if needed
- Prune ground covers if needed
- Train and prune vines if needed
- Harvest herb roots and stems
- Harvest herb leaves and seeds
- Harvest vegetables and fruits when ripe
- Sow seeds outdoors for succession plantings

- Cut flowers for fresh use or drying, but stop dead-heading roses
- Pot bulbs for forcing and begin to chill them
- Plant spring-flowering bulbs
- Rake leaves
- Sow seeds of woody plants and perennials that need stratification outdoors
- Take hardwood cuttings for rooting
- Lay sod; plant plugs
- Mow and edge the lawn as needed
- Thatch and aerate the lawn if needed

Zone 8

- Prepare soil for autumn or spring planting
- Keep the garden free of weeds
- Plant potted perennial and biennial herbs and flowers, roses, shrubs, trees, ground covers, and vines, and B&B shrubs, trees, ground covers, and vines
- Plant bare-root shrubs, trees, ground covers, and vines
- Divide and transplant perennial herbs and flowers and ground covers
- Transplant deciduous trees and shrubs
- Plant hardy annuals

169

- Water as needed

- Spray with insecticides and fungicides if needed

- Prune ground covers if needed

- Train and prune vines if needed

- Harvest herb roots and stems

- Harvest herb leaves and seeds

- Harvest vegetables and fruits when ripe

- Sow seeds outdoors for succession plantings

- Cut flowers for fresh use or drying, but stop dead-heading roses

- Remove and replace spent annual plants

- Pot bulbs for forcing and begin to chill them

- Plant spring-flowering bulbs

- Rake leaves

- Take hardwood cuttings for rooting

- Sow grass seed; lay sod; plant plugs

- Overseed dormant warm-season lawn grass

- Mow and edge the lawn as needed

- Thatch and aerate the lawn if needed

Zone 9

- Prepare soil for autumn or spring planting

- Keep the garden free of weeds

- Plant potted perennial and biennial herbs and flowers, roses, shrubs, trees, ground covers, and vines, and B&B shrubs, trees, ground covers, and vines

- Plant bare-root shrubs, trees, ground covers, and vines

- Divide and transplant perennial herbs and flowers and ground covers

- Transplant deciduous trees and shrubs

- Plant hardy annuals

- Water as needed

- Spray with insecticides and fungicides if needed

- Prune ground covers if needed

- Train and prune vines if needed

- Fertilize the garden as needed

- Harvest herb roots and stems

- Harvest herb leaves and seeds

- Harvest vegetables and fruits when ripe

- Sow seeds outdoors for succession plantings

- Replace spent annuals

- Cut flowers for fresh use or drying

- Plant spring-flowering bulbs

- Pot bulbs for forcing and begin to chill them

- Take hardwood cuttings for rooting

- Sow grass seed; lay sod; plant plugs

- Overseed dormant warm-season lawn grass

- Mow and edge the lawn as needed

- Thatch and aerate the lawn if needed

Zone 10

- Prepare soil for autumn or spring planting

- Keep the garden free of weeds

- Plant potted perennial and biennial herbs and flowers, roses, shrubs, trees, ground covers, and vines, and B&B shrubs, trees, ground covers, and vines

- Plant bare-root shrubs, trees, ground covers, and vines

- Divide and transplant perennial herbs and flowers and ground covers

- Transplant deciduous trees and shrubs

- Water as needed

- Spray with insecticides and fungicides if needed

170

- Prune ground covers if needed

- Train and prune vines if needed

- Fertilize the garden if needed

- Harvest herb roots and stems

- Harvest herb leaves and seeds

- Harvest vegetables and fruit when ripe

- Sow seeds outdoors for succession plantings

- Replace spent annuals

- Cut flowers for fresh use or drying

- Pot bulbs for forcing and begin to chill them

- Sow grass seed; lay sod; plant plugs

- Overseed dormant warm-season lawn grass

- Mow and edge the lawn as needed

- Thatch and aerate the lawn if needed

Zone 11

- Prepare soil for autumn or spring planting

- Keep the garden free of weeds

- Plant potted perennial and biennial herbs and flowers, roses, shrubs, trees, ground covers, and vines, and B&B shrubs, trees, ground covers, and vines

- Plant bare-root shrubs, trees, ground covers, and vines

- Divide and transplant perennial herbs and flowers and ground covers

- Transplant deciduous trees and shrubs

- Water as needed

- Spray with insecticides and fungicides if needed

- Prune ground covers if needed

- Train and prune vines if needed

- Fertilize the garden if needed

- Harvest herb roots and stems

- Harvest herb leaves and seeds

- Harvest vegetables and fruits when ripe

- Sow seeds outdoors for succession plantings

- Replace spent annuals

- Cut flowers for fresh use or drying

- Pot bulbs for forcing and begin to chill them

- Sow grass seed; lay sod; plant plugs

- Overseed dormant warm-season lawn grass

- Mow and edge the lawn as needed

- Thatch and aerate the lawn if needed

N O V E M B E R

1	2	3	4	5	6	7
8	9	10	11	12	13	14
15	16	17	18	19	20	21
22	23	24	25	26	27	28
29	30					

Zone 1

- Check winter protection; add more if necessary

- Order plants for spring planting

- Spray evergreens with antidesiccant

Zone 2

- Check winter protection; add more if necessary

- Order plants for spring planting

- Spray evergreens with antidesiccant

Zone 3

- Check winter protection; add more if necessary

- Order plants for spring planting

- Spray evergreens with antidesiccant

171

Zone 4

- Check winter protection; add more if necessary
- Order plants for spring planting
- Spray evergreens with antidesiccant

Zone 5

- Check winter protection; add more if necessary
- Order plants for spring planting
- Apply dormant fertilizer to trees, shrubs, ground covers, and vines

- Prune shade trees
- Prune fruits between now and late winter
- Cut back tops of spent perennials
- Remove annual flowers, herbs, and vegetables killed by frost
- Plant and mulch very hardy annuals, such as ornamental kale
- Rake leaves
- Harvest vegetables and fruits when ripe
- Spray evergreens with antidesiccant
- Repair and paint trellises, arbors, fences, benches, and garden accessories
- Fertilize the lawn if one feeding is needed, if not done in the spring
- Fertilize the lawn for the second time if two yearly feedings are needed or for the third time if three yearly feedings are needed

Zone 6

- Order plants for spring planting
- Apply dormant fertilizer to trees, shrubs, ground covers, and vines
- Prune shade trees
- Prune fruits between now and late winter

- Apply winter protection
- Plant very hardy annuals, such as ornamental kale
- Cut back tops of spent perennials
- Remove annual flowers, herbs, and vegetables killed by frost
- Rake leaves
- Prepare soil for autumn or spring planting
- Plant bare-root perennial herbs and flowers, roses, trees, shrubs, ground covers, and vines
- Transplant roses
- Plant spring-flowering bulbs
- Dig and store tender bulbs
- Spray evergreens with antidesiccant
- Water evergreens if needed
- Harvest vegetables and fruit when ripe
- Repair and paint trellises, arbors, fences, benches, and garden accessories
- Fertilize the lawn if one feeding is needed, if not done in the spring
- Fertilize the lawn for the second time if two yearly feedings are needed or for the third time if three yearly feedings are needed

172

Zone 7

- Order plants for spring planting

- Apply winter protection

- Cut back tops of spent perennials

- Plant and mulch hardy annuals

- Remove annual flowers, herbs, and vegetables killed by frost

- Rake leaves

- Prepare soil for autumn or spring planting

- Plant bare-root perennial herbs and flowers, roses, trees, shrubs, ground covers, and vines

- Apply dormant fertilizer to trees, shrubs, ground covers, and vines

- Transplant roses

- Prune shade trees

- Prune fruits between now and late winter

- Plant spring-flowering bulbs

- Dig and store tender bulbs

- Spray evergreens with antidesiccant

- Water evergreens if needed

- Harvest vegetables and fruit when ripe

- Repair and paint trellises, arbors, fences, benches, and garden accessories

- Fertilize the lawn if one feeding is needed, if not done in the spring

- Fertilize the lawn for the second time if two yearly feedings are needed or for the third time if three yearly feedings are needed

Zone 8

- Order plants for spring planting

- Apply winter protection

- Cut back tops of spent perennials

- Remove annual flowers, herbs, and vegetables killed by frost

- Plant and mulch hardy annuals

- Rake leaves

- Prepare soil for autumn or spring planting

- Plant potted or bare-root biennial and perennial herbs, flowers, roses, trees, shrubs, ground covers, vines, and B&B shrubs, trees, ground covers, and vines

- Transplant roses and deciduous shrubs and trees

- Prune shade trees

- Prune fruits between now and late winter

- Plant spring-flowering bulbs

- Sow biennial and perennial herb and flower seeds outdoors

- Sow seeds of woody plants outdoors

- Divide and transplant perennial herbs and flowers and ground covers

- Dig and store tender bulbs

- Water plants, if needed, especially evergreens

- Harvest herb roots and stems

- Harvest herb seeds and leaves

- Cut flowers for fresh use or drying

- Lay sod; plant plugs

- Overseed dormant warm-season lawn grass

- Mow and edge the lawn as needed

173

- Fertilize the lawn if one feeding is needed, if not done in the spring

- Fertilize the lawn for the second time if two yearly feedings are needed or for the third time if three yearly feedings are needed

Zone 9

- Order plants for spring planting

- Cut back tops of spent perennials

- Remove annuals killed by frost

- Plant hardy and half-hardy annual flower and vegetable seeds and transplants outdoors

- Sow seeds outdoors for succession plantings

- Rake leaves

- Prepare soil for autumn or spring planting

- Plant potted or bare-root biennial and perennial herbs, flowers, roses, trees, shrubs, ground covers, vines, and B&B shrubs, trees, ground covers, and vines

- Plant spring-flowering bulbs

- Sow biennial and perennial herb and flower seeds outdoors

- Sow seeds of woody plants outdoors

- Divide and transplant perennial herbs and flowers and ground covers

- Prune shade trees

- Prune fruits between now and late winter

- Prune ground covers if needed

- Train and prune vines if needed

- Dig and store tender bulbs

- Fertilize plants if needed

- Water plants if needed

- Withhold water from established plants to induce dormancy

- Harvest herb roots and stems

- Harvest herb seeds and leaves

- Harvest vegetables and fruits when ripe

- Cut flowers for fresh use or drying

- Spray with insecticides and fungicides if needed

- Keep the garden free of weeds

- Lay sod; plant plugs

- Overseed dormant warm-season lawn grass

- Mow and edge the lawn as needed

- Fertilize the lawn if one feeding is needed, if not done in the spring

- Fertilize the lawn for the second time if two yearly feedings are needed or for the third time if three yearly feedings are needed

Zone 10

- Plant tender bulbs

- Replace spent annuals

- Order plants for spring planting

- Cut back tops of spent perennials

- Plant flower and vegetable seeds and transplants outdoors

- Sow seeds outdoors for succession plantings

- Rake leaves

- Prepare soil for autumn or spring planting

- Plant potted or bare-root biennial and perennial herbs, flowers, roses, trees, shrubs, ground covers, vines, and B&B shrubs, trees, ground covers, and vines

- Sow biennial and perennial herb and flower seeds outdoors

- Sow seeds of woody plants outdoors

- Divide and transplant perennial herbs and flowers and ground covers

- Prune shade trees

- Prune fruits between now and late winter

- Prune ground covers if needed

- Train and prune vines if needed

- Fertilize plants if needed

- Water plants if needed

174

- Withhold water from established plants to induce dormancy
- Harvest herb roots and stems
- Harvest herb seeds and leaves
- Harvest vegetables and fruits when ripe

- Cut flowers for fresh use or drying
- Spray with insecticides and fungicides if needed
- Keep the garden free of weeds
- Lay sod; plant plugs

- Overseed dormant warm-season lawn grass
- Mow and edge the lawn as needed
- Fertilize the lawn if one feeding is needed, if not done in the spring
- Fertilize the lawn for the second time if two yearly feedings are needed or for the third time if three yearly feedings are needed

Zone 11

- Plant tender bulbs
- Replace spent annuals
- Order plants for spring planting
- Cut back tops of spent perennials
- Plant flower and vegetable seeds and transplants outdoors
- Sow seeds outdoors for succession plantings
- Rake leaves
- Prepare soil for autumn or spring planting
- Plant potted or bare-root biennial and perennial herbs, roses, trees, shrubs, ground covers, vines, and B&B shrubs, trees, ground covers, and vines
- Sow biennial and perennial herb and flower seeds outdoors
- Sow seeds of woody plants outdoors

- Divide and transplant perennial herbs and flowers and ground covers
- Prune shade trees
- Prune fruits between now and late winter
- Prune ground covers if needed
- Train and prune vines if needed
- Fertilize plants if needed
- Water plants if needed
- Withhold water from established plants to induce dormancy
- Harvest herb roots and stems
- Harvest herb seeds and leaves
- Harvest vegetables and fruits when ripe
- Cut flowers for fresh use or drying
- Spray with insecticides and fungicides if needed
- Keep the garden free of weeds
- Lay sod; plant plugs
- Overseed dormant warm-season lawn grass
- Mow and edge the lawn as needed
- Fertilize the lawn if one feeding is needed, if not done in spring
- Fertilize the lawn for the second time if two yearly feedings are needed or for the third time if three yearly feedings are needed

175

Winter

DECEMBER

1	2	3	4	5	6	7
8	9	10	11	12	13	14
15	16	17	18	19	20	21
22	23	24	25	26	27	28
29	30	31				

Zone 1

- Pot tender bulbs for indoor bloom
- Order plants and seeds for spring
- Clean, sharpen, and oil tools; sharpen mower blades
- Remove snow and ice from evergreens

Zone 2

- Pot tender bulbs for indoor bloom
- Order plants and seeds for spring
- Clean, sharpen, and oil tools; sharpen mower blades
- Remove snow and ice from evergreens

Zone 3

- Pot tender bulbs for indoor bloom
- Order plants and seeds for spring
- Clean, sharpen, and oil tools; sharpen mower blades
- Remove snow and ice from evergreens

Zone 4

- Pot tender bulbs for indoor bloom
- Order plants and seeds for spring
- Clean, sharpen, and oil tools; sharpen mower blades
- Remove snow and ice from evergreens

Zone 5

- Pot tender bulbs for indoor bloom
- Order plants and seeds for spring
- Clean, sharpen, and oil tools; sharpen mower blades
- Remove snow and ice from evergreens

Zone 6

- Pot tender bulbs for indoor bloom

- Order plants and seeds for spring
- Clean, sharpen, and oil tools; sharpen mower blades
- Remove snow and ice from evergreens

Zone 7

- Pot tender bulbs for indoor bloom
- Order plants and seeds for spring
- Clean, sharpen, and oil tools; sharpen mower blades
- Prune shade trees
- Remove snow and ice from evergreens
- Spray evergreens with antidesiccant

Zone 8

- Pot tender bulbs for indoor bloom
- Order plants and seeds for spring
- Prepare soil for planting
- Plant potted or bare-root perennial herbs, flowers, roses, shrubs, trees, ground covers, and vines, and B&B shrubs, trees, ground covers, and vines
- Divide and transplant perennial herbs and flowers and ground covers

177

- Transplant roses, shrubs, and trees

- Prune shade trees

- Apply dormant fertilizer to trees, shrubs, ground covers, and vines

- Apply winter protection

- Sow seeds of hardy annual flowers and vegetables indoors

- Sow tender annual and vegetable seeds indoors that require 12 weeks or more

- Clean, sharpen, and oil tools; sharpen mower blades

- Spray evergreens with antidesiccant

- Repair and paint trellises, arbors, fences, benches, and garden accessories

Zone 9

- Pot tender bulbs for indoor bloom

- Refrigerate hardy bulbs that require chilling

- Order plants and seeds for spring

- Prepare soil for planting

- Plant potted or bare-root perennial herbs, flowers, roses, shrubs, trees, ground covers, and vines, and B&B shrubs, trees, ground covers, and vines

- Divide and transplant perennial herbs and flowers and ground covers

- Remove annuals killed by frost

- Transplant roses, shrubs, and trees

- Prune shade trees

- Prune ground covers if needed

- Train and prune vines if needed

- Fertilize plants if needed

- Sow seeds of hardy annual vegetables, herbs, and flowers indoors

- Sow biennial and perennial herb and flower seeds indoors or outdoors

- Sow seeds of tender annual flowers and vegetables that require 12 weeks or more indoors

- Plant hardy and half-hardy seeds and transplants outdoors

- Clean, sharpen, and oil tools; sharpen mower blades

- Water as needed

- Spray with insecticides and pesticides if needed

- Harvest herb roots and stems

- Harvest herb leaves and seeds

- Cut flowers for fresh use or drying

- Repair and paint trellises, arbors, fences, benches, and garden accessories

- Lay sod; plant plugs

- Overseed dormant warm-season grass

- Mow and edge the lawn if needed

Zone 10

- Plant tender bulbs

- Pot tender bulbs for indoor bloom

- Refrigerate hardy bulbs that require chilling

- Order plants and seeds for spring

- Prepare soil for planting

- Plant potted or bare-root perennial herbs, flowers, roses, shrubs, trees, ground covers, and vines, and B&B shrubs, trees, ground covers, and vines

- Divide and transplant perennial herbs and flowers and ground covers

- Transplant roses, shrubs, and trees

- Prune shade trees

- Prune ground covers if needed

- Train and prune vines if needed

- Fertilize plants if needed

- Keep the garden free of weeds

- Sow seeds of hardy annual vegetables, herbs, and flowers indoors

178

- Sow biennial and perennial herb and flower seeds indoors or outdoors

- Sow seeds of tender annual flowers and vegetables indoors

- Plant hardy and half-hardy seeds and transplants outdoors

- Clean, sharpen, and oil tools; sharpen mower blades

- Water plants if needed

- Spray with insecticides and pesticides if needed

- Harvest herb roots and stems

- Harvest herb leaves and seeds

- Cut flowers for fresh use or drying

- Repair and paint trellises, arbors, fences, benches, and garden accessories

- Lay sod; plant plugs

- Overseed dormant warm-season grass

- Mow and edge the lawn if needed

Zone 11

- Plant tender bulbs

- Pot tender bulbs for indoor bloom

- Refrigerate hardy bulbs that require chilling

- Order plants and seeds for spring

- Prepare soil for planting

- Plant potted or bare-root perennial herbs, flowers, roses, shrubs, trees, ground covers, and vines, and B&B shrubs, trees, ground covers, and vines

- Divide and transplant perennial herbs and flowers and ground covers

- Transplant roses, shrubs, and trees

- Prune shade trees

- Prune ground covers if needed

- Train and prune vines if needed

- Fertilize plants if needed

- Keep the garden free of weeds

- Sow seeds of hardy annual vegetables, herbs, and flowers indoors

- Sow biennial and perennial herb and flower seeds indoors or outdoors

- Sow seeds of tender annual flowers and vegetables indoors

- Plant hardy and half-hardy seeds and transplants outdoors

- Clean, sharpen, and oil tools; sharpen mower blades

- Water plants if needed

- Spray with insecticides and pesticides if needed

- Harvest herb roots and stems

- Harvest herb leaves and seeds

- Cut flowers for fresh use or drying

- Repair and paint trellises, arbors, fences, benches, and garden accessories

- Lay sod; plant plugs

- Overseed dormant warm-season grass

- Mow and edge the lawn if needed

179

JANUARY

1	2	3	4	5	6	7
8	9	10	11	12	13	14
15	16	17	18	19	20	21
22	23	24	25	26	27	28
29	30	31				

Zone 1

- Check winter mulch and replace if needed
- Press heaved plants back into the soil
- Study mail-order catalogs
- Order seeds, bulbs, and plants for spring
- Pot and chill bulbs for forcing
- Move chilled bulbs indoors for forcing
- Spray broad-leaved evergreens with antidesiccant
- Remove snow and ice from evergreens
- Avoid walking on frozen lawns

Zone 2

- Check winter mulch and replace if needed
- Press heaved plants back into the soil
- Study mail-order catalogs
- Order seeds, bulbs, and plants for spring
- Pot and chill bulbs for forcing
- Move chilled bulbs indoors for forcing
- Spray broad-leaved evergreens with antidesiccant
- Remove snow and ice from evergreens
- Avoid walking on frozen lawns

Zone 3

- Check winter mulch and replace if needed
- Press heaved plants back into the soil
- Study mail-order catalogs
- Order seeds, bulbs, and plants for spring
- Pot and chill bulbs for forcing
- Move chilled bulbs indoors for forcing
- Spray broad-leaved evergreens with antidesiccant
- Remove snow and ice from evergreens
- Avoid walking on frozen lawns

Zone 4

- Check winter mulch and replace if needed
- Press heaved plants back into the soil
- Study mail-order catalogs
- Order seeds, bulbs, and plants for spring
- Pot and chill bulbs for forcing
- Move chilled bulbs indoors for forcing
- Spray broad-leaved evergreens with antidesiccant
- Remove snow and ice from evergreens
- Avoid walking on frozen lawns

Zone 5

- Check winter mulch and replace if needed
- Press heaved plants back into the soil
- Study mail-order catalogs
- Order seeds, bulbs, and plants for spring
- Pot and chill bulbs for forcing
- Move chilled bulbs indoors for forcing
- Sow hardy and half-hardy annual flower, vegetable, and herb seeds indoors

180

- Sow seeds of tender annuals that require 12 weeks or more indoors

- Spray broad-leaved evergreens with antidesiccant

- Remove snow and ice from evergreens

- Avoid walking on frozen lawns

Zone 6

- Check winter mulch and replace if needed

- Press heaved plants back into the soil

- Study mail-order catalogs

- Order seeds, bulbs, and plants for spring

- Pot and chill bulbs for forcing

- Move chilled bulbs indoors for forcing

- Sow hardy and half-hardy annual flower, vegetable, and herb seeds indoors

- Sow seeds of tender annuals that require 12 weeks or more indoors

- Spray broad-leaved evergreens with antidesiccant

- Remove snow and ice from evergreens

- Avoid walking on frozen lawns

Zone 7

- Check winter mulch and replace if needed

- Press heaved plants back into the soil

- Study mail-order catalogs

- Order seeds, bulbs, and plants for spring

- Pot and chill bulbs for forcing

- Move chilled bulbs indoors for forcing

- Sow hardy and half-hardy annual flower, vegetable, and herb seeds indoors

- Sow seeds of tender annuals that require 12 weeks or more indoors

- Spray broad-leaved evergreens with antidesiccant

- Remove snow and ice from evergreens

- Avoid walking on frozen lawns

Zone 8

- Check winter mulch and replace if needed

- Press heaved plants back into the soil

- Study mail-order catalogs

- Order seeds, bulbs, and plants for spring

- Pot and chill bulbs for forcing

- Move chilled bulbs indoors for forcing

- Sow perennial and biennial flower and herb seeds indoors

- Sow seeds of tender annuals and vegetables that require 8 to 10 weeks indoors

- Sow seeds of hardy and half-hardy annual flowers and vegetables indoors

- Spray broad-leaved evergreens with antidesiccant

- Remove snow and ice from evergreens

- Avoid walking on frozen lawns

Zone 9

- Study mail-order catalogs

- Order seeds, bulbs, and plants for spring

- Plan and design the garden

- Apply mulch if frost is forecast

- Press heaved plants back into the soil

- Pot and chill bulbs for forcing

- Move chilled bulbs indoors for forcing

- Prepare soil for spring planting

- Test soil pH; adjust if necessary

- Plant refrigerated bulbs outdoors

181

- Sow annual, biennial, and perennial flower, vegetable, and herb seeds indoors or outdoors

- Plant potted or bare-root roses, shrubs, trees, perennial flowers, vines, ground covers, and herbs, and B&B shrubs, trees, vines, and ground covers

- Transplant hardy and half-hardy seedlings outdoors

- Train and prune vines

- Prune roses, ground covers, shade trees, and summer- and autumn-flowering shrubs and trees

- Fertilize roses after pruning

- Fertilize shrubs, trees, ground covers, vines, fruits, and perennial flowers and herbs as growth starts

- Water if needed

- Spray dormant shrubs and trees with horticultural oil

- Divide and transplant perennial herbs and summer- and autumn-blooming perennial flowers

- Transplant roses, shrubs, trees, ground covers, and vines

- Thin overcrowded perennials and ground covers

- Harvest herb leaves and seeds

- Cut flowers for fresh use or drying

- Sow grass seed; lay sod; plant plugs

- Mow and edge the lawn if needed

Zone 10

- Study mail-order catalogs

- Order seeds, bulbs, and plants for spring

- Plan and design the garden

- Pot and chill bulbs for forcing

- Move chilled bulbs indoors for forcing

- Prepare soil for spring planting

- Test soil pH; adjust if necessary

- Plant refrigerated bulbs outdoors

- Plant tender bulbs

- Fertilize early flowering bulbs

- Spray with insecticides and fungicides if needed

- Spray dormant shrubs and trees with horticultural oil

- Sow annual, biennial, and perennial herb, vegetable, and flower seeds indoors or out-doors

- Plant potted or bare-root roses, shrubs, trees, ground covers, vines, herbs, and flowering perennials, and B&B shrubs, trees, vines, and ground covers

- Transplant seedlings outdoors

- Prune roses, shade trees, ground covers, and summer- and autumn-flowering shrubs and trees

- Train and prune vines

- Fertilize roses after pruning

- Fertilize shrubs, trees, ground covers, vines, fruits, and peren-nial herbs and flowers as growth starts

- Water if needed

- Divide and transplant perennial herbs and summer- and autumn-blooming perennial flowers

- Transplant roses, shrubs, trees, ground covers, and vines

- Thin overcrowded perennials, herbs, and ground covers

- Keep the garden free of weeds

- Harvest herb leaves and seeds

- Harvest vegetables and fruits when ripe

- Cut flowers for fresh use or drying

- Sow grass seed; lay sod; plant plugs

- Mow and edge the lawn as needed

Zone 11

- Study mail-order catalogs

- Order seeds, bulbs, and plants for spring

- Plan and design the garden

- Pot and chill bulbs for forcing

- Move chilled bulbs indoors for forcing

- Prepare soil for spring planting

- Test soil pH; adjust if necessary

- Plant refrigerated bulbs out-doors

- Plant tender bulbs

- Fertilize early flowering bulbs

- Spray with insecticides and fungicides if needed

- Spray dormant shrubs and trees with horticultural oil

- Sow annual, biennial, and perennial herb, vegetable, and flower seeds indoors or outdoors

- Plant potted or bare-root roses, shrubs, trees, ground covers, vines, herbs, and perennial flowers, and B&B shrubs, trees, ground covers, and vines

- Transplant seedlings outdoors

- Prune roses, ground covers, shade trees, and summer- and autumn-flowering shrubs and trees

- Train and prune vines

- Fertilize roses after pruning

- Fertilize shrubs, trees, ground covers, vines, perennial herbs, fruits, and flowers as growth starts

- Water if needed

- Divide and transplant perennial herbs and summer- and autumn-blooming flowers

- Transplant roses, shrubs, trees, ground covers, and vines

- Thin overcrowded perennials, herbs, and ground covers

- Keep the garden free of weeds

- Harvest herb leaves and seeds

- Cut flowers for fresh use or drying

- Sow grass seed; lay sod; plant plugs

- Mow and edge the lawn

183

FEBRUARY

1	2	3	4	5	6	7
8	9	10	11	12	13	14
15	16	17	18	19	20	21
22	23	24	25	26	27	28

Zone 1

- Check winter mulch and add more if needed
- Press heaved plants back into the soil
- Study mail-order catalogs
- Order bulbs, seeds, and plants for spring
- Sow tender annual seeds that require 12 weeks or more indoors
- Plan and design the garden
- Place chilled bulbs indoors for forcing
- Prune shade trees
- Remove snow and ice from evergreens
- Avoid walking on frozen lawns

Zone 2

- Check winter mulch and add more if needed

- Press heaved plants back into the soil
- Study mail-order catalogs
- Order bulbs, seeds, and plants for spring
- Sow tender annual seeds that require 12 weeks or more indoors
- Plan and design the garden
- Place chilled bulbs indoors for forcing
- Prune shade trees
- Remove snow and ice from evergreens
- Avoid walking on frozen lawns

Zone 3

- Check winter mulch and add more if needed
- Press heaved plants back into the soil
- Study mail-order catalogs
- Order bulbs, seeds, and plants for spring
- Sow tender annual seeds indoors that require 12 weeks or more indoors
- Plan and design the garden
- Place chilled bulbs indoors for forcing
- Prune shade trees
- Remove snow and ice from evergreens

- Avoid walking on frozen lawns

Zone 4

- Check winter mulch and add more if needed
- Press heaved plants back into the soil
- Study mail-order catalogs
- Order bulbs, seeds, and plants for spring
- Plan and design the garden
- Place chilled bulbs indoors for forcing
- Sow hardy and half-hardy annual and vegetable seeds indoors
- Sow tender annual and vegetable seeds that require 12 weeks or more indoors
- Prune shade trees
- Remove snow and ice from evergreens
- Avoid walking on frozen lawns

Zone 5

- Check winter mulch and add more if needed
- Press heaved plants back into the soil
- Study mail-order catalogs
- Order bulbs, seeds, and plants for spring
- Plan and design the garden

184

- Sow tender annual and vegetable seeds that require 8 to 12 weeks indoors
- Place chilled bulbs indoors for forcing
- Sow hardy and half-hardy annual and vegetable seeds indoors
- Prune shade trees
- Remove snow and ice from evergreens
- Avoid walking on frozen lawns

Zone 6

- Check winter mulch and add more if needed
- Press heaved plants back into the soil
- Study mail-order catalogs
- Order bulbs, seeds, and plants for spring
- Plan and design the garden
- Place chilled bulbs indoors for forcing
- Sow hardy and half-hardy annual and vegetable seeds indoors
- Sow tender annual and vegetable seeds that require 6 to 8 weeks indoors
- Prune shade trees
- Remove snow and ice from evergreens
- Avoid walking on frozen lawns

Zone 7

- Check winter mulch and add more if needed
- Press heaved plants back into the soil
- Study mail-order catalogs
- Order bulbs, seeds, and plants for spring
- Plan and design the garden
- Place chilled bulbs indoors for forcing
- Sow hardy and half-hardy annual and vegetable seeds indoors
- Sow tender annual and vegetable seeds that require 6 to 8 weeks indoors
- Prune shade trees
- Remove snow and ice from evergreens
- Avoid walking on frozen lawns

Zone 8

- Remove winter protection as growth starts
- Study mail-order catalogs
- Order bulbs, seeds, and plants for spring
- Plan and design the garden
- Fertilize early flowering bulbs
- Prepare soil for planting
- Test soil pH; adjust if necessary

- Sow perennial and biennial herb and flower seeds indoors and outdoors
- Sow tender annual seeds that require 4 to 6 weeks indoors
- Sow seeds of woody plants indoors or outdoors
- Sow hardy and half-hardy annual seeds outdoors
- Plant potted or bare-root roses, shrubs, trees, ground covers, vines, and perennial and biennial herbs and flowers, and B&B shrubs, trees, ground covers, and vines
- Transplant hardy and half-hardy seedlings outdoors
- Fertilize shrubs, trees, ground covers, vines, and perennial herbs, fruits, and flowers as growth starts
- Transplant roses, shrubs, trees, ground covers, and vines
- Prune roses, shade trees, ground covers, and summer- and autumn-flowering shrubs and trees
- Prune and train vines
- Fertilize roses after pruning
- Water if needed
- Spray with insecticides and fungicides if needed
- Apply horticultural oil to dormant shrubs and trees

185

- Divide and transplant ground covers, perennial herbs, and summer- and autumn-blooming perennial flowers

- Thin overcrowded ground covers, herbs, and perennial flowers

- Root chrysanthemum cuttings

Zone 9

- Study mail-order catalogs

- Order bulbs, seeds, and plants for spring

- Plant refrigerated bulbs outdoors

- Plant tender bulbs outdoors

- Prepare soil for planting

- Test soil pH; adjust if necessary

- Sow annual, perennial, and biennial herb, vegetable, and flower seeds indoors and outdoors

- Sow seeds of woody plants indoors or outdoors

- Plant potted or bare-root roses, shrubs, trees, ground covers, vines, and annual, perennial, and biennial herbs and flowers, and B&B shrubs, trees, ground covers, and vines

- Transplant seedlings outdoors

- Protect tender plants from unexpected frosts

- Fertilize perennial herbs and flowers as growth starts

- Transplant roses, shrubs, trees, ground covers, and vines

- Prune shade trees, ground covers, and summer- and autumn-flowering shrubs and trees

- Train and prune vines

- Apply summer mulch

- Water plants if needed

- Fertilize early flowering bulbs

- Start tubers, rhizomes, and tuberous roots indoors

- Plant forced bulbs outdoors

- Spray with insecticides and fungicides if needed

- Divide and transplant perennial herbs, ground covers, and summer- and autumn-blooming perennial flowers

- Thin overcrowded herbs, ground covers, and perennial flowers

- Harvest herb leaves and seeds

- Cut flowers for fresh use or drying

- Root chrysanthemum cuttings

- Take softwood cuttings of woody plants for rooting

- Layer stems and vines for propagating

- Sow grass seed; lay sod; plant plugs

- Mow and edge the lawn as needed

- Fertilize the lawn if one yearly feeding is needed, if not done in late autumn

Zone 10

- Study mail-order catalogs

- Order bulbs, seeds, and plants for spring

- Plant refrigerated bulbs outdoors

- Plant tender bulbs outdoors

- Water plants if needed

- Fertilize early flowering bulbs

- Start tubers, rhizomes, and tuberous roots indoors

- Plant forced bulbs outdoors

- Prepare soil for planting

- Test soil pH; adjust if necessary

- Sow annual, perennial, and biennial herb, vegetable, and flower seeds indoors and outdoors

- Sow seeds of woody plants indoors or outdoors

- Plant potted or bare-root roses, shrubs, trees, ground covers, vines, and annual, perennial, and biennial herbs and flowers, and B&B shrubs, trees, ground covers, and vines

- Transplant seedlings outdoors

- Fertilize perennial herbs and flowers as growth starts

- Transplant roses, shrubs, trees, ground covers, and vines

- Prune shade trees, ground covers, and summer- and autumn-flowering shrubs and trees

- Train and prune vines

- Apply summer mulch

- Spray with insecticides and fungicides if needed

- Divide and transplant perennial herbs, ground covers, and summer- and autumn-blooming perennial flowers

- Thin overcrowded herbs, ground covers, and perennial flowers; thin seedlings

- Harvest herb leaves and seeds

- Harvest vegetables and fruits when ripe

- Cut flowers for fresh use or drying

- Root chrysanthemum cuttings

- Take softwood cuttings of woody plants for rooting

- Layer stems and vines for propagating

- Sow grass seed; lay sod; plant plugs

- Mow and edge the lawn as needed

- Fertilize the lawn if one yearly feeding is needed, if not done in late autumn

Zone 11

- Study mail-order catalogs

- Order bulbs, seeds, and plants for spring

- Plant refrigerated bulbs outdoors

- Plant tender bulbs outdoors

- Water plants if needed

- Fertilize early flowering bulbs

- Start tubers, rhizomes, and tuberous roots indoors

- Plant forced bulbs outdoors

- Prepare soil for planting

- Test soil pH; adjust if needed

- Sow annual, perennial, and biennial herb, vegetable, and flower seeds indoors and outdoors

- Sow seeds of woody plants indoors or outdoors

- Plant potted or bare-root roses, shrubs, trees, ground covers, vines, and annual, perennial, and biennial herbs and flowers, and B&B shrubs, trees, ground covers, and vines

- Transplant seedlings outdoors

- Fertilize perennial herbs and flowers as growth starts

- Transplant roses, shrubs, trees, ground covers, and vines

- Apply summer mulch

- Prune shade trees, ground covers, and summer- and autumn-flowering shrubs and trees

- Train and prune vines

- Spray with insecticides and fungicides if needed

- Divide and transplant perennial herbs, ground covers, and summer- and autumn-flowering perennial flowers

- Thin overcrowded herbs, perennial flowers, and ground covers; thin seedlings

- Harvest herb leaves and seeds

- Harvest vegetables and fruits when ripe

- Cut flowers for fresh use or drying

- Root chrysanthemum cuttings

- Take softwood cuttings of woody plants for rooting

- Layer stems and vines for propagating

- Sow grass seed; lay sod; plant plugs

- Mow and edge the lawn as needed

- Fertilize the lawn if one yearly feeding is needed, if not done in late autumn

187

AVERAGE DATES
OF LAST
SPRING FROST

May 30 or after
April 30 to May 30
March 30 to April 30
February 28 to March 30
January 30 to February 28
January 30 or before

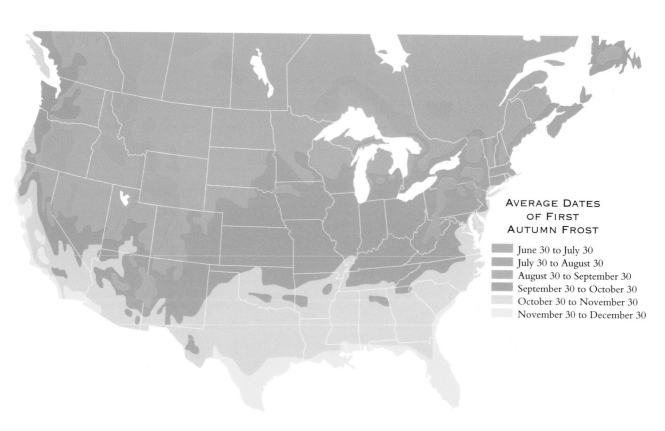

AVERAGE DATES
OF FIRST
AUTUMN FROST

June 30 to July 30
July 30 to August 30
August 30 to September 30
September 30 to October 30
October 30 to November 30
November 30 to December 30

188

REGIONAL WARM-SEASON, COOL-SEASON LAWN MAP

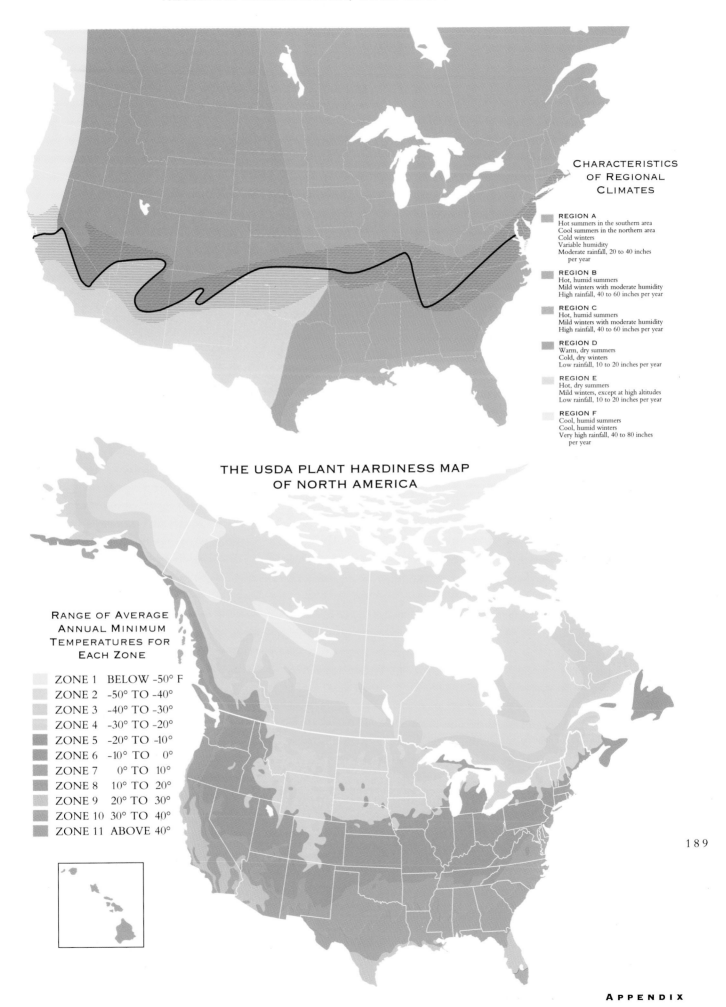

CHARACTERISTICS OF REGIONAL CLIMATES

REGION A
Hot summers in the southern area
Cool summers in the northern area
Cold winters
Variable humidity
Moderate rainfall, 20 to 40 inches
per year

REGION B
Hot, humid summers
Mild winters with moderate humidity
High rainfall, 40 to 60 inches per year

REGION C
Hot, humid summers
Mild winters with moderate humidity
High rainfall, 40 to 60 inches per year

REGION D
Warm, dry summers
Cold, dry winters
Low rainfall, 10 to 20 inches per year

REGION E
Hot, dry summers
Mild winters, except at high altitudes
Low rainfall, 10 to 20 inches per year

REGION F
Cool, humid summers
Cool, humid winters
Very high rainfall, 40 to 80 inches
per year

THE USDA PLANT HARDINESS MAP OF NORTH AMERICA

RANGE OF AVERAGE
ANNUAL MINIMUM
TEMPERATURES FOR
EACH ZONE

ZONE 1   BELOW -50° F
ZONE 2   -50° TO -40°
ZONE 3   -40° TO -30°
ZONE 4   -30° TO -20°
ZONE 5   -20° TO -10°
ZONE 6   -10° TO   0°
ZONE 7   0° TO 10°
ZONE 8   10° TO 20°
ZONE 9   20° TO 30°
ZONE 10   30° TO 40°
ZONE 11 ABOVE 40°

189

191

PHOTOGRAPHY CREDITS

192